Self-Publishing on a ZERO Budget

How To Publish eBooks and Paperbacks With NO Money

Ava Fails

© 2017 Ava Fails All Rights Reserved. This book or any portion thereof may not be reproduced or used in any manner whatsoever without the express written permission of the publisher except for the use of brief quotations in a book review.

SELF-PUBLISHING ON A ZERO BUDGET

Table of Contents

Introduction 4
    What You Will Need 4
    What You Will Learn 5
Writing and Preparing Your Manuscript 7
    Wrapping Up The Manuscript 12
Editing, Proofreading, and Cover Creation 14
    The Proofreading Process 14
    The Editing Process 15
    Creating a Cover for Your E-book 16
    How Did Our Cover Turn Out? 29
Uploading Your Manuscript to Kindle Direct Publishing 31
    Kindle eBook Details 32
    Kindle eBook Content 43
    Kindle eBook Pricing 48
Createspace - Publishing in Paperback 52
    Before We Get Started 52
    Createspace vs. KDP Paperback 52
    Publishing with Createspace 53
        Title Information 55
        ISBN 56
        Interior 58
        Cover 70
        Complete Setup 82
        Channels 84
        Pricing 87

Managing Your Royalties 89

   Getting Paid from Kindle Direct Publishing (KDP) 89
   Checking Your Royalty Reports in KDP 91
   Getting Paid from Createspace 93
   Checking Your Royalty Reports in Createspace 95
   What You Should Expect for Tax Time 96

Marketing Your Book 98

   Examples From My Experience 98
   What is the Goal of Your Book? 100
   Marketing Elements to Include in Your Manuscript 101
   Marketing Your Book Before and After Launch 101
      Speaking of Pen Names 106
   Benefits of Permafree Books 106
      The Caveat of Permafree 107
   Being Active in Your Niche 108
   Your Author Website 108
   Kindle Direct Publishing Marketing Tools 109
      Paid Marketing 109

That's the End! 111

Introduction

You're probably reading this book because you want to self-publish your books, but you're broke or you just don't want to spend money to do it.

I'm here to tell you that it's possible, and I'll show you exactly how to prepare, format, and self-publish your manuscript in both eBook and paperback on Amazon and beyond.

Rather than investing money in your self-publishing endeavors, you will invest your time instead. If you have a good handle on writing and using Word, you should have the skills needed to do everything in this book.

For the best results, I suggest that you scan through this full book before you get started.

What You Will Need

- A Google Account
- A Kindle Direct Publishing Account - This is easy, just go to **https://kdp.amazon.com/** and sign in with your existing Amazon account. If you don't have an Amazon account, you will need to create one.
- An existing manuscript - If you have one, you're a few

steps ahead, if not, you'll need to go through the writing process and come back to this

- A Canva.com account
- Your cover in JPG format - we'll create this in this tutorial
- A description of your book in 4000 characters or less - You will be required to type a description when you upload your manuscript to KDP, whether you do it beforehand or on the fly is up to you. **Here's a character counter for your convenience.**
- A Createspace account - **https://www.createspace.com/**
- A bank account
- Your tax information
- A smattering of social media accounts and a website will greatly help with your book marketing

What You Will Learn

- How to write/format your manuscript using free tools
- How to edit with ZERO budget
- How to proofread with ZERO budget
- How to create a book cover with, you guessed it, ZERO budget

- How to upload your files to KDP and create your book listing
- How to determine royalties and pricing
- How to select categories
- About Kindle Select
- How to convert your Kindle cover to work with Createspace
- How to publish in print
- Createspace vs. KDP Paperback
- How to set up your KDP and Createspace accounts so you can get paid
- How to check the reports available on your accounts
- How to make your book free on Amazon
- How market your book for free
- What not to do

Writing and Preparing Your Manuscript

The reason you need a Google account is that we are going to be using Google Docs to create/format your manuscript.

Why not Word, you ask?

Word is a bit too complicated for the level of formatting we need.

With Google Docs, you can jump right in without having to set up styles, etc. To access Google Docs, log into your Google account and use your browser to navigate to https://drive.google.com/.

In case you weren't aware, this is your Google Drive and you have 15GB of free cloud storage space attached to your account. This is great for self-publishers because it creates a backup of your work in the cloud. It also autosaves every time you make a change to your document.

Step 1. Open a new document by clicking **New** and selecting **Google Docs** from the drop-down menu.

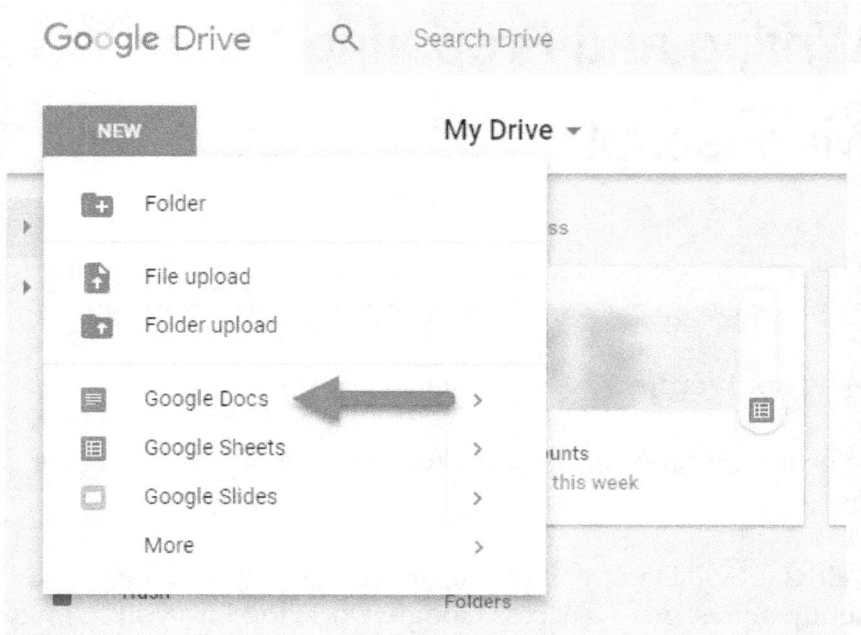

Step 2. Create your Title Page using the **Title** and **Subtitle** (if you have one) styles. Also, type the Title of your working file by clicking in the **Untitled Document** area.

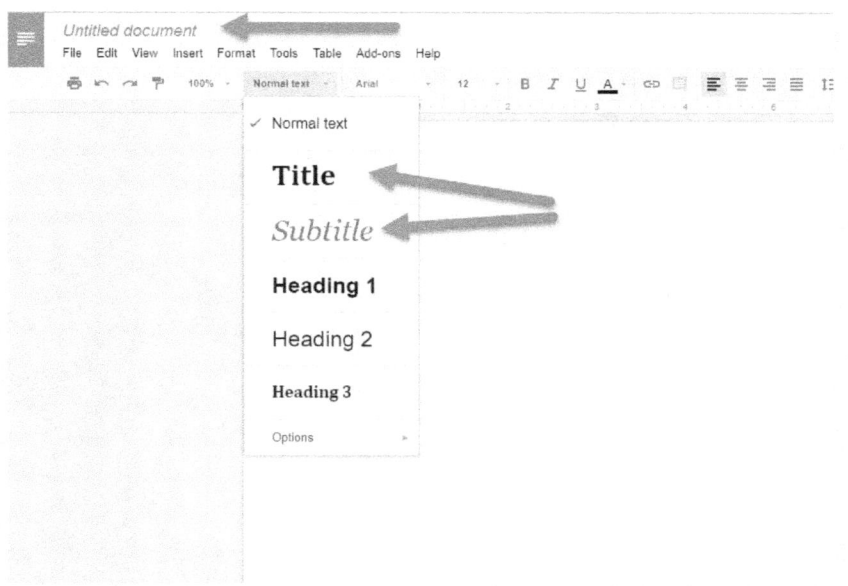

Step 3. You will probably want to insert a generic copyright statement at the bottom of your title page. Perhaps something like this:

> *Copyright © 2017 Your Name All rights reserved. This book or any portion thereof may not be reproduced or used in any manner whatsoever without the express written permission of the publisher except for the use of brief quotations in a book review.*

Your book is copyrighted merely by the act of your creating it. You can register a copyright officially for about $35; however, this is not a requirement or even really necessary. Get more information at - http://www.copyright.gov/

Step 4. Insert a **Page Break** once your Title Page is complete. You can either press **Ctrl Enter** or click **Insert** and select **Page Break** from the drop-down menu.

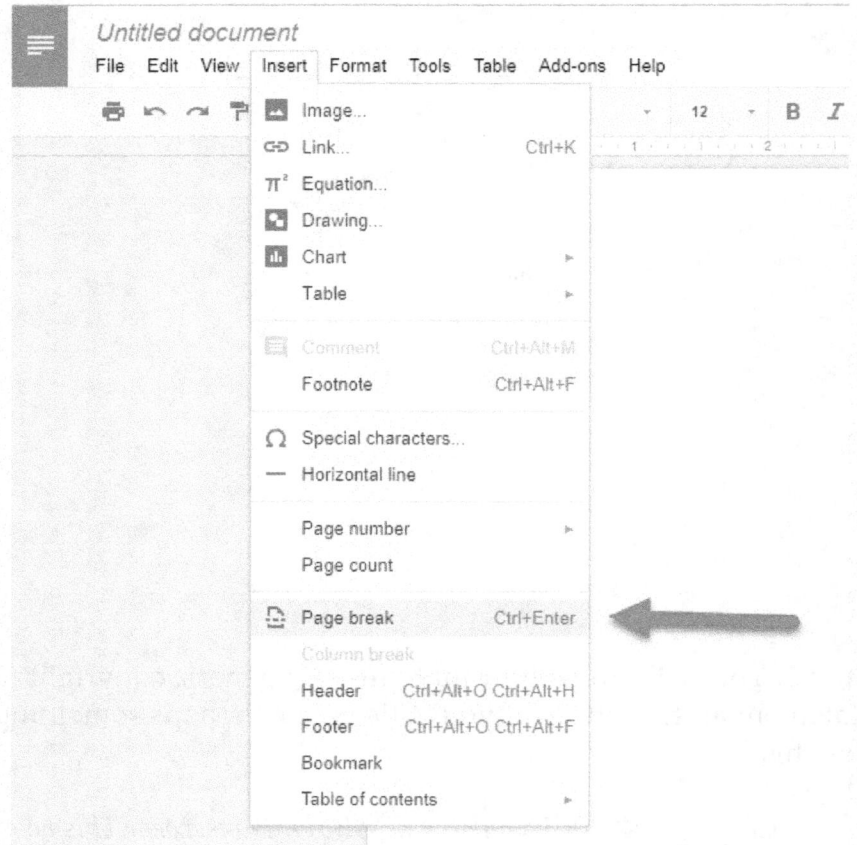

Step 5. Use the **Heading 1** style for all of your Chapter headings and other pages you include such as a Dedication, Foreward, Preface, etc.

NOTE: If you adjust any of the font sizes, say for Headings or Title, do NOT make them more than 20 pt. This will make them display incorrectly in smaller format devices.

Step 6. Write the body of your chapters using the **Normal text** style. If you have already written your book, and you are just formatting, make sure there is consistency with your styles.

All Headings should use the Heading 1 style and all body text should be Normal text and have the same font size and type. The most simple way is probably to set the entire document to Normal text with a consistent font size and type. Then go through and format your Headings.

Step 7. Insert Page Breaks after each chapter.

Step 8. Create a Table of Contents at the beginning of your manuscript, usually by inserting a new Page Break after the Title page. Then click **Insert** and select **Table of contents** from the drop-down menu.

NOTE: You can easily update your TOC by right-clicking it at the top and selecting **Update table of contents** near the bottom of the fly-out menu.

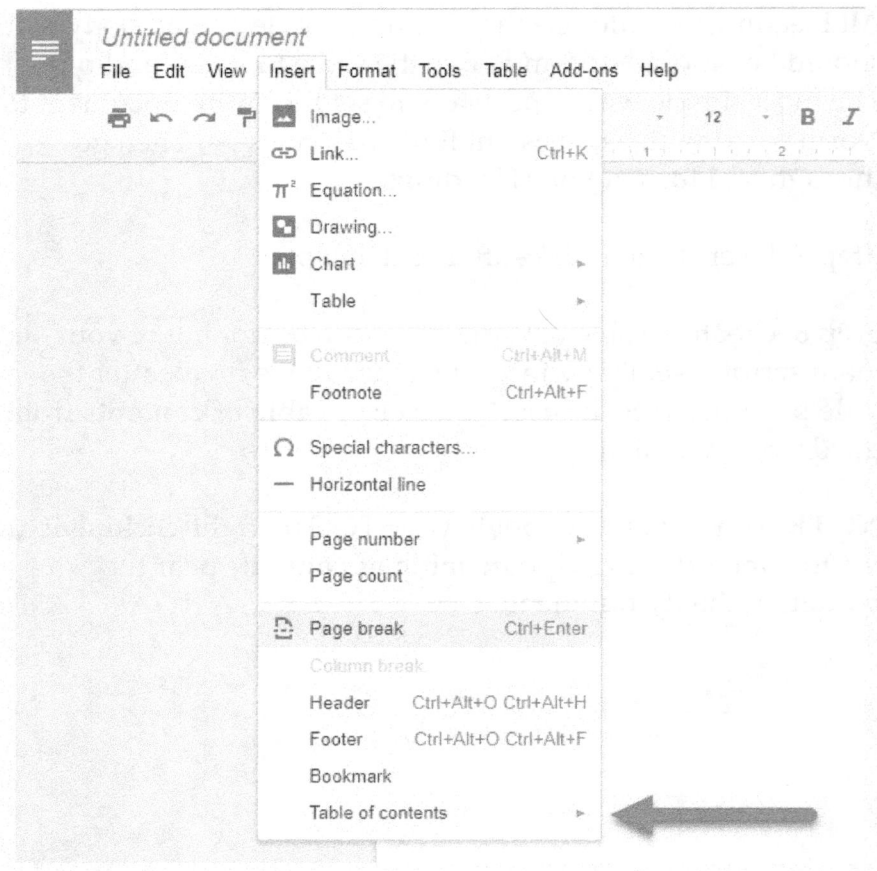

Wrapping Up The Manuscript

Once you have formatted your entire manuscript using these simple steps. You are done. Do not make your formatting more complicated than it needs to be. Do not EVER use the **Tab** key when formatting for Kindle as it will really cause problems for you. Use the **First Line Indent** instead if you insist on more complicated formatting.

The final step is to download your manuscript as a Word document by clicking **File**, hover your cursor over **Download as** and select **Word document** from the fly-out menu.

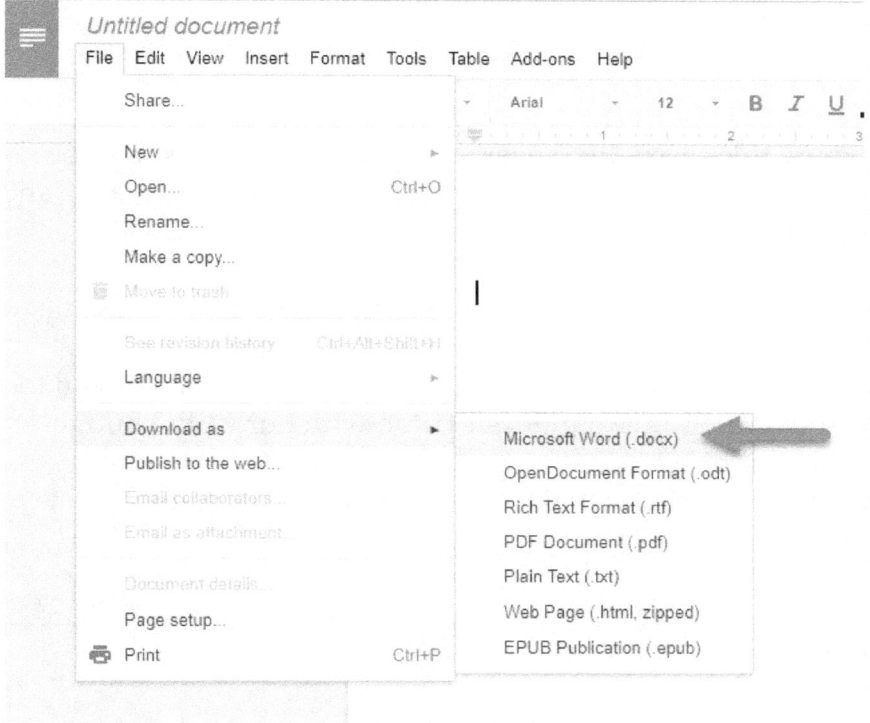

This will be the file that you upload to KDP.

Editing, Proofreading, and Cover Creation

I know this seems like several steps in one and it is, but the editing and proofreading process doesn't take many steps and is simple to explain.

Let me preface my editing and proofreading tips by saying:

Most professional authors and self-publishers will tell you to hire an editor, but that doesn't fit in with our ZERO budget. I've never hired an editor for my work, and it probably needed it, but I still make consistent passive income regardless.

I edit client books using the same system I'm about to share with you.

The Proofreading Process

Readers tend to notice typos and grammar mistakes before they see editing errors or problems with flow. If you are a writer with any experience under your belt, then you know how difficult it can be to proof and edit your own material.

If you are proofreading your work yourself, these 5 steps will help you catch most of the errors:

1. As you write, proofread each paragraph as you complete it.
2. Proofread your previous day's work, when you sit down to write for the day. At this point, you have proofed each paragraph and each section of writing you've completed.
3. Scan the manuscript as a whole for any spelling errors picked up by your editing program (look for the squiggly red lines).
4. Proofread the entire manuscript.

The Editing Process

I would suggest letting your manuscript sit for a few days after you finish writing it before you begin the editing process. I have had manuscripts I let sit for YEARS...it's not like they expire or spoil. You will be editing and proofing right from Google Docs. It will autosave your edits.

The idea here is to look on the work with a fresh perspective. Here is my 3-step editing process:

1. Go through and edit for flow. Add that thing you forgot. Elaborate in certain spots. Whatever you feel enhances your story for the reader.

2. Go through a second time backwards, one sentence at a time. Yes, I'm serious.

3. Let it sit again and go through one final time to catch anything you might have missed.

TIP: If you have friends or family who enjoy your writing and have decent editing or proofing skills, you can always get them to take a look at your work in exchange for the chance to read it before anyone else.

I actually created an email list of "beta readers" from Facebook for this purpose. They proofread for me and leave me a review in exchange for reading my book for free.

When you complete these steps, you've proofread your manuscript 4 times and edited it 3 times. Call it good.

Don't forget to re-download your Word file. Delete the old one.

Creating a Cover for Your E-book

I don't want you to feel intimidated here. Your cover is important and people DO judge books by the cover, but it is possible to create a great cover for your book without being a professional designer.

If you don't already have one, create a Canva account. You can sign in with your existing Facebook or Google account or create your account with your email address and password. It's totally FREE.

Canva creates a crazy amount of different graphics and documents. You may very well find it useful for other things in addition to book cover creation.

Step 1. Click the + icon if you don't see **Kindle Cover** in the frequently-used items across the top of your account.

You will find the **Kindle Cover** under the **Blogging and eBooks** heading.

Step 2. Click **Kindle Cover** to begin designing. It will open in a new browser tab.

There will be a number of examples in the **Layouts** tab to the left of your workspace. I always design from scratch, but if you choose one of these, know that your cover may not be exclusive or original to your book.

Also, you have to watch the items you use in this space from all tabs. Some of them are paid items. Free items are annotated with **Free** as shown below. Don't worry, a good amount of the elements on Canva are free to use. If you can't find something, you can upload your own to the platform.

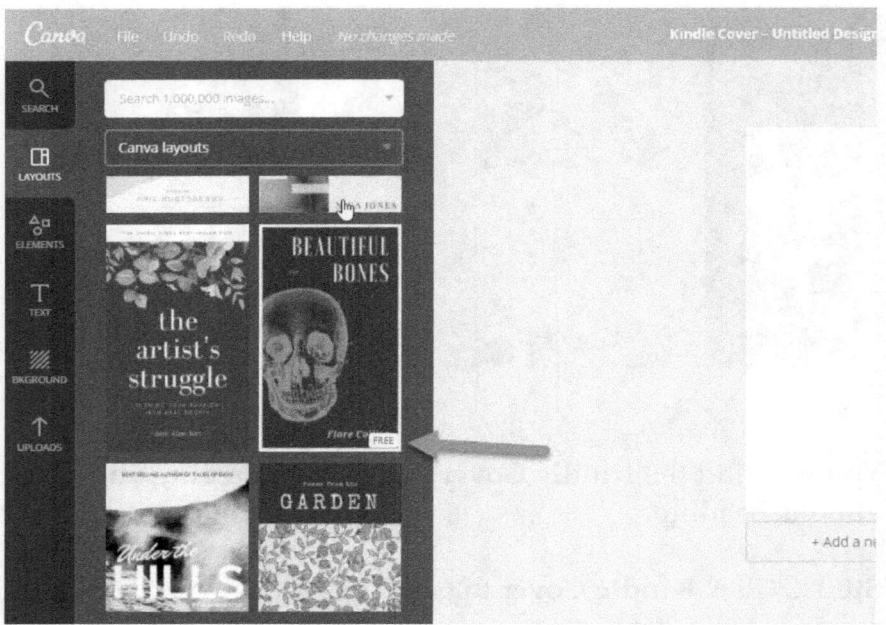

Step 3. Let's do some research. We want to take a look at the best sellers in the Kindle Store on Amazon.

Click **Kindle eBooks** in the left navigation.

AVA FAILS

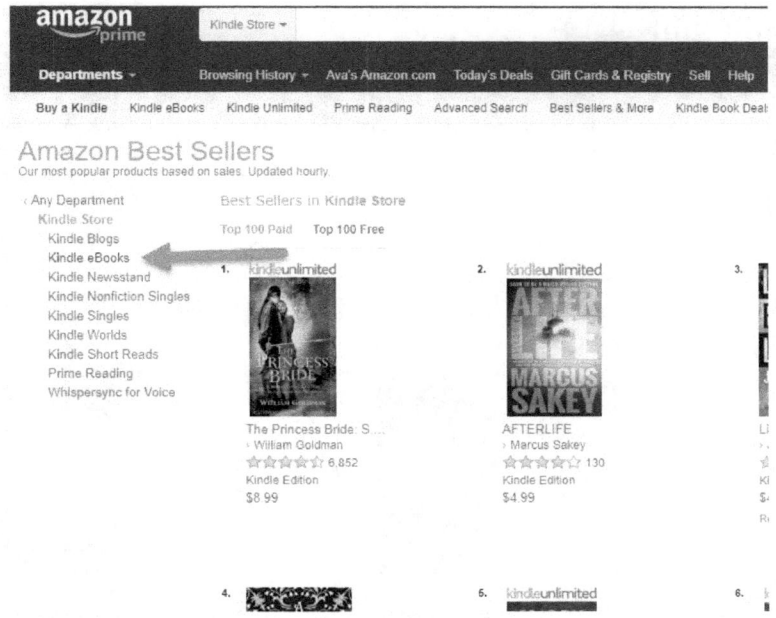

This opens a huge list of genres that go well beyond what my screen shot can show:

Find your genre.

I chose **Mystery, Thriller, & Suspense** to use as an example.

There's a couple things you should notice here:

1. Selecting a genre opens up a list of sub-genres beneath it most of the time. Explore until you have been as specific as possible with your own book.
2. There are two lists available to you here: the **Top 100 Paid** and the **Top 100 Free**.

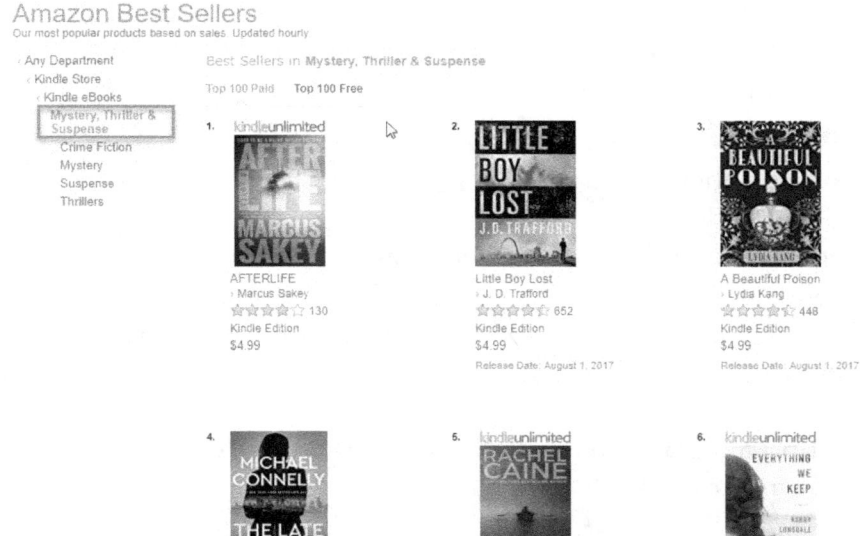

We will be concentrating on the **Top 100 Paid** list, but it's worthy to note here that you can get TONS of free books by perusing the **Top 100 Free** lists, as well as check out what your competition is putting out. Also, there is one of each of these lists for each genre and sub-genre.

Scroll through the **Top 100 Paid** list for your genre and take note of the book covers. Which ones do you like? Which ones do you think would fit your book and be simple to replicate? If you would like to save a few examples, just click onto the sales page for the book on Amazon and right-click; **Save Image as**.

NOTE: By "replicate" I don't mean copy. I mean create something similar.
These are actual covers of books that are already selling well. Use them as examples. Pay attention to things like:

- The large, easy-to-read fonts. You can easily read the

title and most of the time, the author even on the small thumbnails
- Colors
- Images
- Simplicity

I wouldn't consider these cover designs to be really complicated. Most of them consist of one simple image making up the entire background of the cover with large, plain fonts.

Let's find an example to work with as if we are creating a cover for our book.

From my example, **I chose the #4 listing as of this writing for Stillhouse Lake by Rachel Caine.** Here's the cover:

Note: We are NOT copying Rachel's cover. We are using the ideas and elements to create our own.

I like this cover because of its simplicity, the colors, and the large, plain fonts.

Let's pretend that we are publishing a book titled Faded Sky by Jane Doe. The loose storyline is about a pilot who disappeared with his/her plane without a trace. So, we are sticking to our Mystery, Thriller, & Suspense genre.

Step 4. Find a suitable stock/royalty-free image to use. You can try searching your keyword on a free image site like Pixabay or Pexels. I like to just use Google and filter my search so that I'm searching multiple free image sites at once.

Type your keyword into Google. Select **Images** to perform an image search. Click the **Tools** button. Click **Usage** and select **Labeled for reuse** from the drop-down menu.

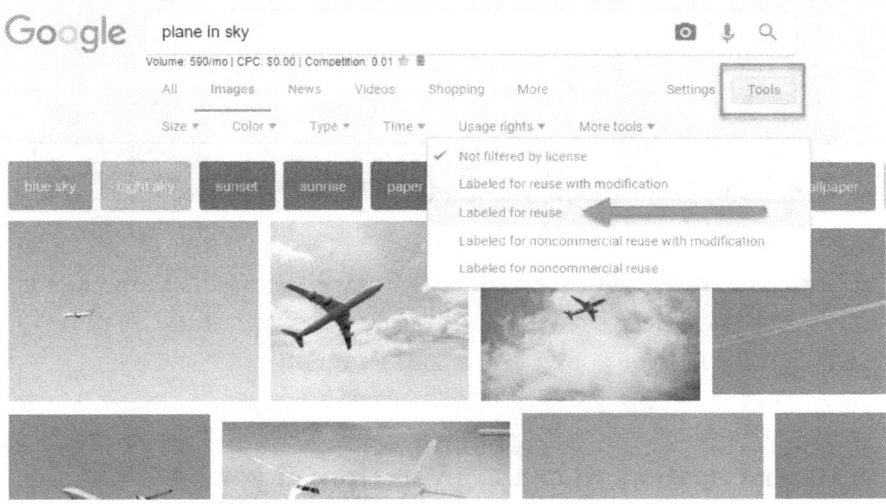

I found this image on Pexels through the above search that is suitable for my cover:

SELF-PUBLISHING ON A ZERO BUDGET

When you find a picture you like, visit the site and check the licensing to make sure you can use it commercially. If you can't, you'll have to select one that you can.

Step 5. Upload your image to Canva. Click the **Uploads** tab in the left navigation. Click the green **Upload your own images** button. The image will upload to Canva.

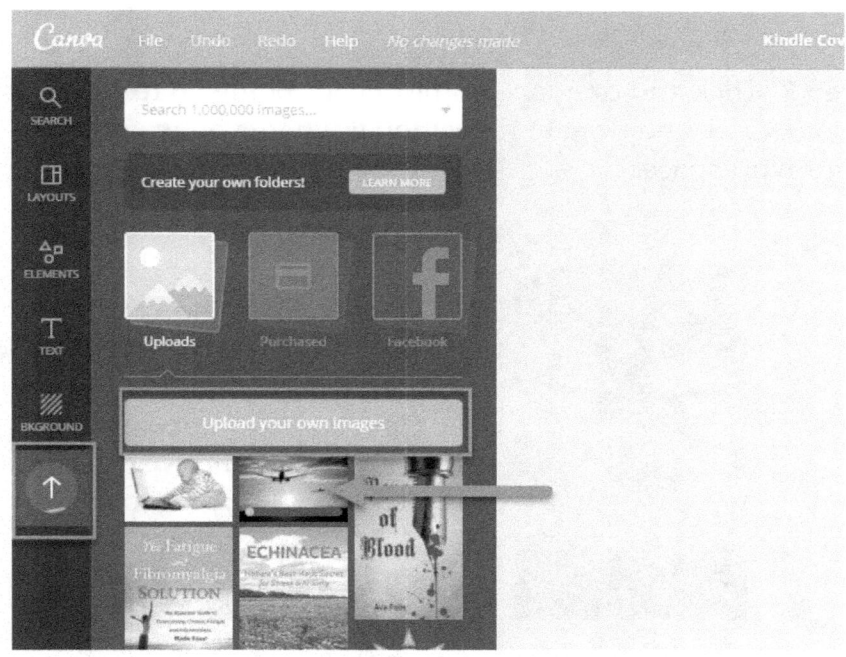

Step 6. Use the uploaded image in your design by clicking it. The image will be added to your workspace. You can see it is selected and surrounded by anchor points so that you can resize it.

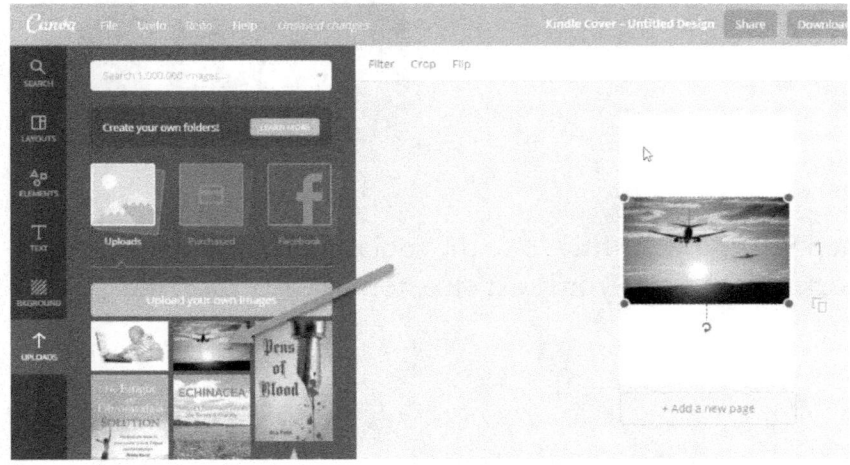

Step 7. Click and drag one of the anchor points to resize your photo. Click and drag to reposition it where you want it in your workspace.

Here's what we have so far:

Step 8. Click the **Text** tab in the left navigation. Click **Add Heading**. The Add Heading text box now appears in the workspace and we can edit it for size, font, and color.

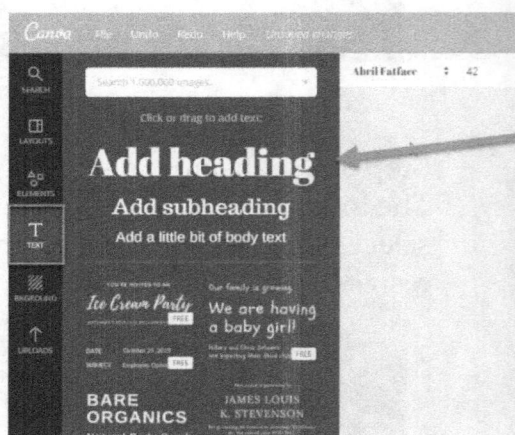

Step 9. Type your title. Use the tools across the top of your workspace to edit your text size, font, style, color, etc.

TIP: I use a browser extension in Chrome called Colorzilla to match the colors in my photo to color my fonts.

To add a custom color in Canva:

- Click **Colorzilla** and hover your cursor over the color you want to match. Click. Colorzilla will automatically copy the 6-digit hex code to your clipboard.
- With your text element selected, click the colored square in the toolbar above. Click the + icon.

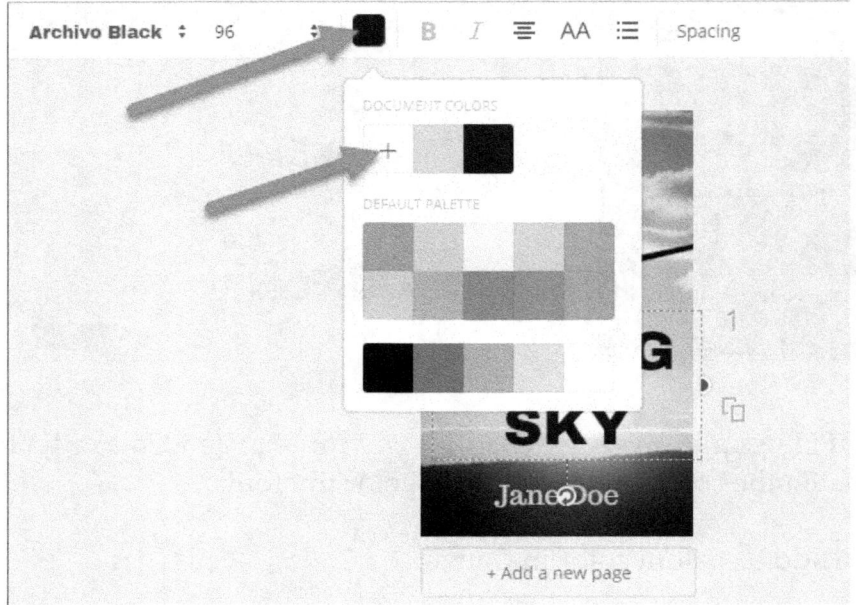

- Paste the 6-digit hex code from Colorzilla into the box.

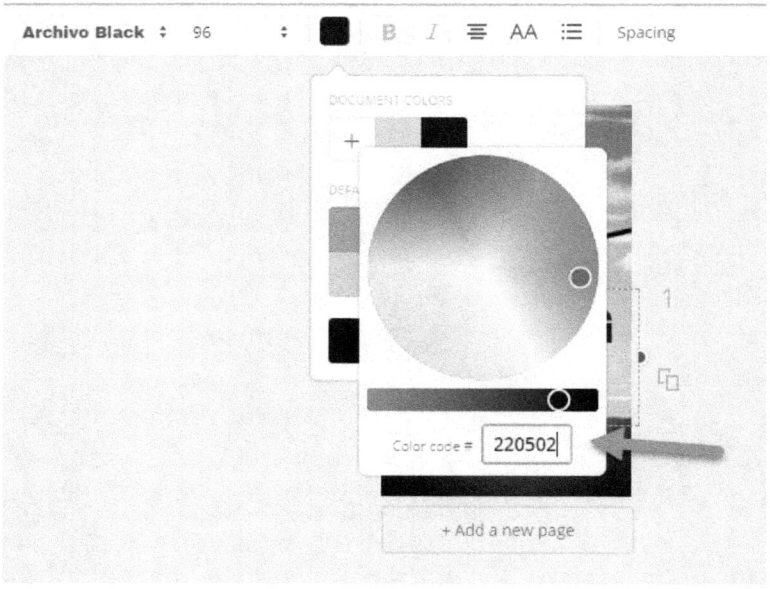

Step 10. Repeat the process for your author name.

Make sure you are pleased at this point with how your cover looks and where everything is placed.

Step 11. Download your cover in JPG format.

Click **Download** in the top bar. Select **JPG** from the drop-down menu. Click the green **Download** button.

Your cover will download to your computer.

NOTE: Feel free to download your cover in any other format as well. JPG is what you will need to upload with your manuscript to KDP and other platforms.

How Did Our Cover Turn Out?

So how does our cover look?

I don't think it's too shabby and it was super simple to make, right? Just an image and a couple lines of text.

Uploading Your Manuscript to Kindle Direct Publishing

Are You Ready?

Today is the day. You become a published author once you complete this process. How does it feel? Great, right?

Let's do this!

Step 1. Log into KDP.

Your dashboard should default to your **Bookshelf**, but if not, click the Bookshelf tab in the navigation at the top of the page.

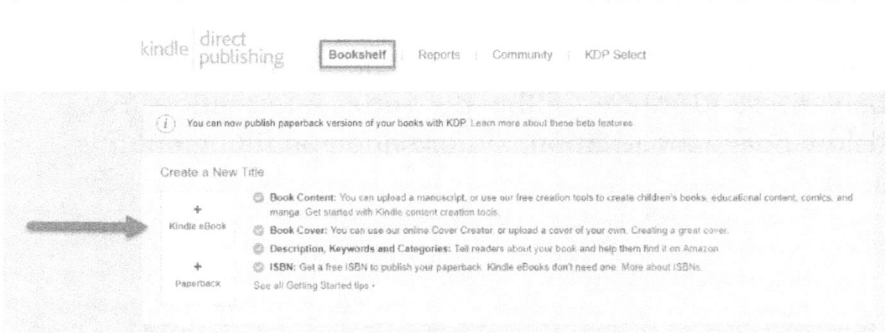

Step 2. Click the **+ Kindle eBook** button as indicated in the image above. At the top of the page, you'll see that KDP breaks up your eBook listing into 3 sections:
- Kindle eBook details

- Kindle eBook content
- Kindle eBook pricing

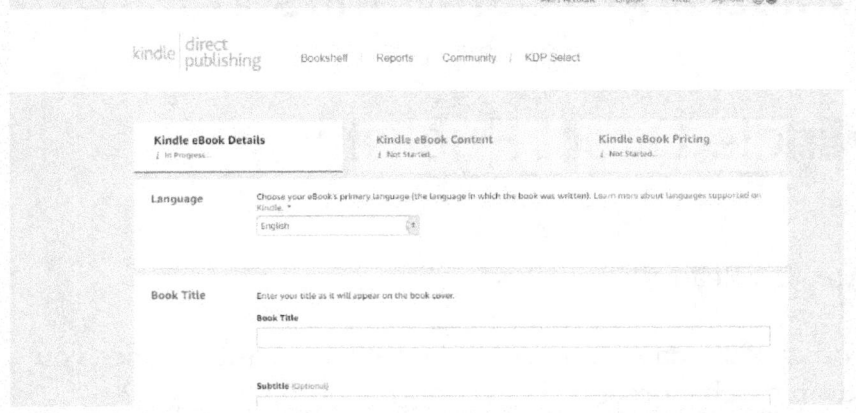

NOTE: I'm going to run through each section step-by-step.

Kindle eBook Details

Step 3. Select the language your book is written in. Type your book title and subtitle. Fill in the **Series** information. (See below image for additional information on filling out this section.)

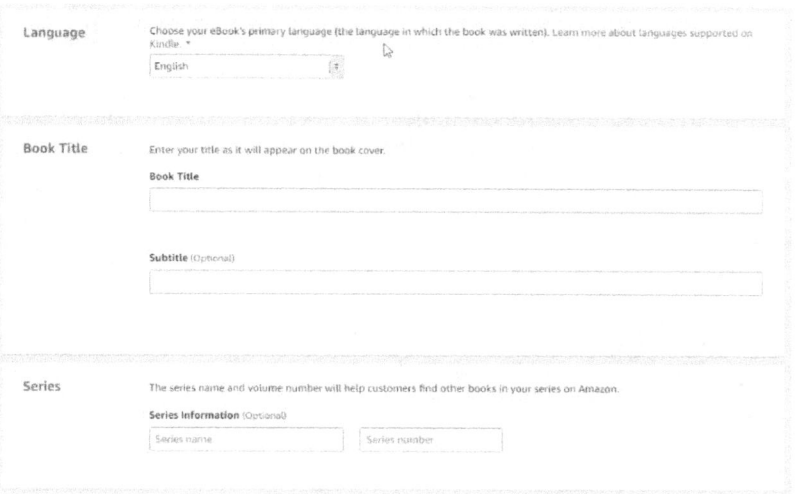

Select your language using the simple drop-down menu.

Type the title of your book in Title case.

Type the subtitle.

This is optional. If your book doesn't have a subtitle, leave this blank. I suggest always including a subtitle that includes your keyword or gives more information about the topic of your book, but I don't recommend keyword stuffing like in this example:

SELF-PUBLISHING ON A ZERO BUDGET

The information you include about your book should always be for the reader to give them additional information on your work. None of these sections are intended for gaming the Amazon algorithm and using them in that manner will only cause you problems later on.

If your book will be a Series, type the name of your Series and "Book 1" or just "1" to indicate where the current title you're listing fits in that Series.
Step 4. Type the Edition number. Type the first and last names of the primary author. Enter information about anyone who contributed to your book. (More information below the image.)

AVA FAILS

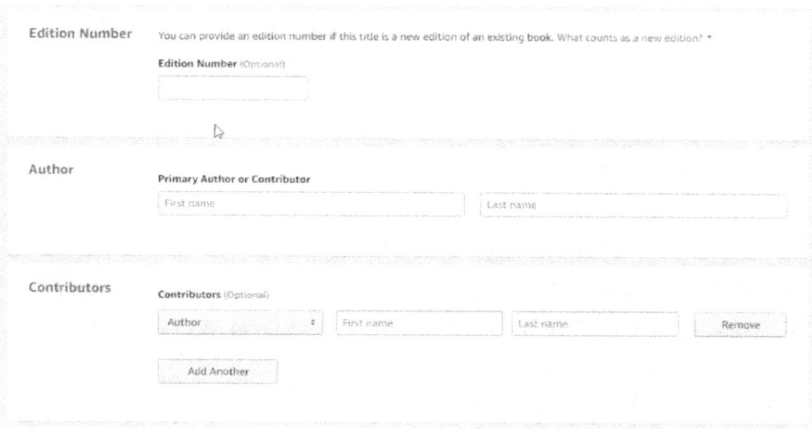

The **Edition** number is optional, but I usually put 1 in the chance that I make revisions to my book later on. At that point, I would enter 2 and so on.
Type your first and last name or that of your pen name into the **Primary Author** or **Contributor** fields.

Contributors are also optional and since the focus of this series is on a ZERO budget, I assume you don't have any. For future reference, this is where you can credit your Editor, Translator, Illustrator or any other contributor you would like.

Step 5. Type the description of your book. Click the radio button to indicate your publishing rights. (More info below image.)

Type your description in 4000 characters or less. A pre-written description comes in handy here. You can simply copy and paste it into the text box.

Writing a book description can be an entire course in and of itself. It's not unlike writing an SEO article for the web. The most important thing to keep in mind when writing your book description is that this is a very significant selling tool for your book. It needs to be clear, concise, and informative.

Include copy that will make them want to buy the book to see more. Don't keyword stuff, write this for the reader only.

Click the radio button to indicate your publishing rights. Ideally, this will be the first one.

Step 6. Type 7 keywords pertaining to your book. (More info after image.)

Again, keywords are more than just a passing thought. These terms are what pulls up your book in the Amazon search results. I'm going to use our example from above.

Remember, we created a fake book idea so we could create a cover. Fading Sky is about a pilot who disappears into thin air and fits into the **Mystery, Thriller, and Suspense** genre.

My method for choosing keywords is simple. I go to the Kindle Store and I type keywords pertaining to my book into the search box and let the auto-suggest help me. These are terms that people are already typing into Amazon to find books.

Let's try it with our example.

What I typed:	What Amazon Suggested:
missing air	missing airplane
airplane	airplane books
	airplane thrillers
	airplane fiction
aviation	aviation thrillers
	aviation books
	aviation fiction
	aviation adventure

There are my 7 keywords and one to grow on!

What you should NOT include in your keywords:

- Another author's name (or anyone's name for that matter)
- Another author's book title
- Brands

Here's more from Amazon about keywords.

Step 7. Set your categories. (More info after image.)

Categories — Choose up to two browse categories. Why are categories important?

[Set Categories]

Ugh, my least favorite part!

As you gain more experience with Kindle Direct Publishing, you will notice a few things. With categories, you will notice that your book is often listed in categories you didn't set. You will also find it nearly impossible to look at a book on Amazon in your genre and be able to match its categories through this publishing process.

HOT TIP: You can get your book in up to 8 additional categories by looking at books in your genre and copying the path to finding their book. You can then use the KDP Contact Us link in your Dashboard to ask that these categories be added. They almost always oblige.

Product details

File Size: 1219 KB
Print Length: 372 pages
Page Numbers Source ISBN: 0451412656
Simultaneous Device Usage: Unlimited
Publisher: Phoenix Flying, Inc. (December 13, 2013)
Publication Date: December 13, 2013
Sold by: Amazon Digital Services LLC
Language: English
ASIN: B009WQ9YMS
Text-to-Speech: Enabled
X-Ray: Enabled
Word Wise: Enabled
Lending: Enabled
Screen Reader: Supported
Enhanced Typesetting: Enabled
Amazon Best Sellers Rank: #194 Paid in Kindle Store (See Top 100 Paid in Kindle Store)
  #1 in Kindle Store > Kindle eBooks > Mystery, Thriller & Suspense > Mystery > **Series**
  #2 in Books > Mystery, Thriller & Suspense > Thrillers & Suspense > **Legal**
  #5 in Kindle Store > Kindle eBooks > Mystery, Thriller & Suspense > Thrillers > **Legal**

Would you like to tell us about a lower price?

KDP uses the BISAC Subject Headings List for categories which is pretty much the standard for the publishing industry.

Figuring out where your book fits is pretty much trial and error. Luckily, we only have to figure out two categories. Let's use our example and see what we can find.

In our case, we will click the + next to **Fiction** to view the sub-categories.

SELF-PUBLISHING ON A ZERO BUDGET

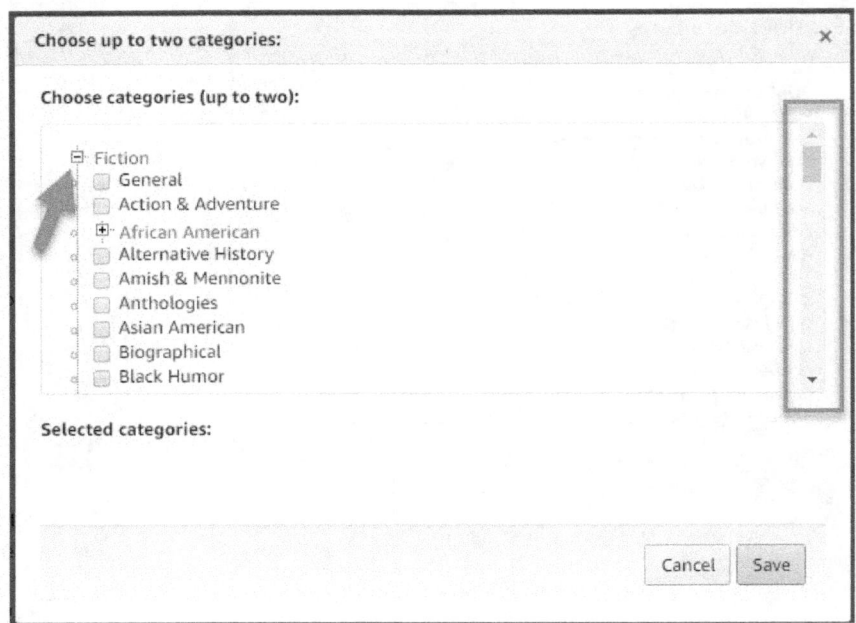

So in keeping with our **Mystery, Thriller and Suspense** genre, I scroll to **M** in the list. Right away, you will notice that these categories also do NOT match the genres on Amazon. I'm stuck with **Mystery & Detective**.

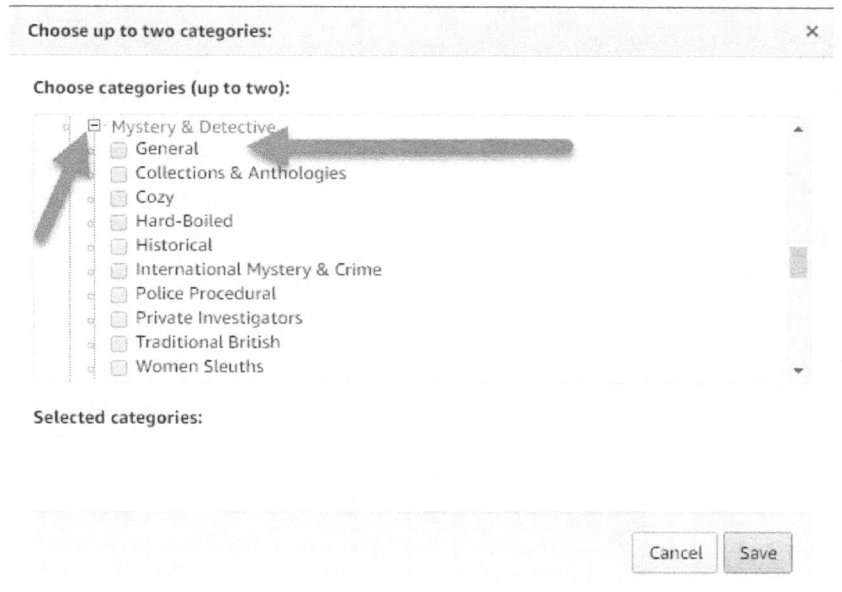

I'm going to go with **General** here since none of the others seem to fit my example. What is **Hard-Boiled**, ha!?!

If I scroll down a little more, I run into the **Thrillers**. I'm going to choose **Suspense** here. You can see how my previous selection was added at the bottom of the window under **Selected Categories**.

SELF-PUBLISHING ON A ZERO BUDGET

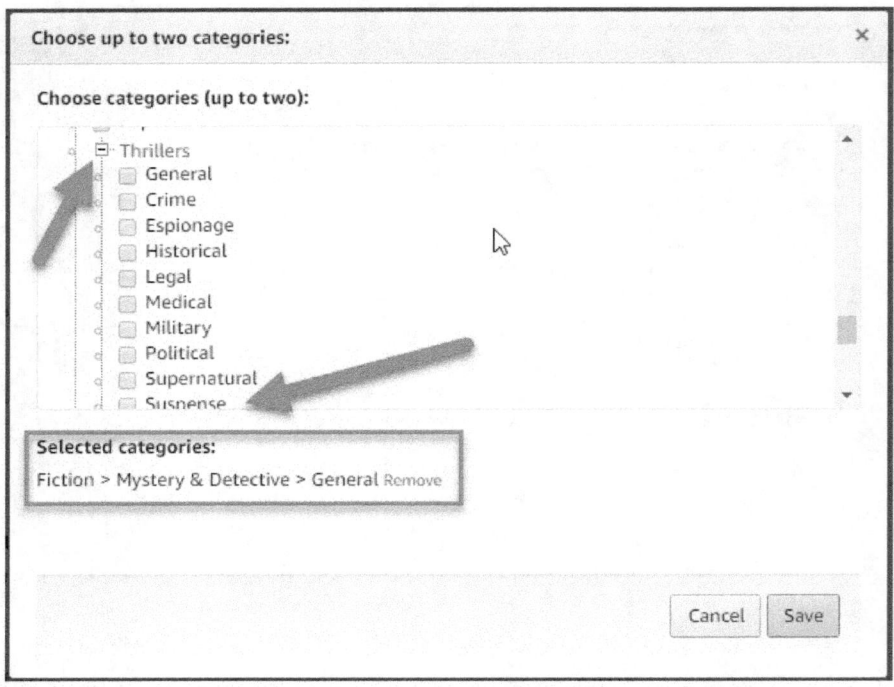

Once you've selected your 2 categories, click **Save**.

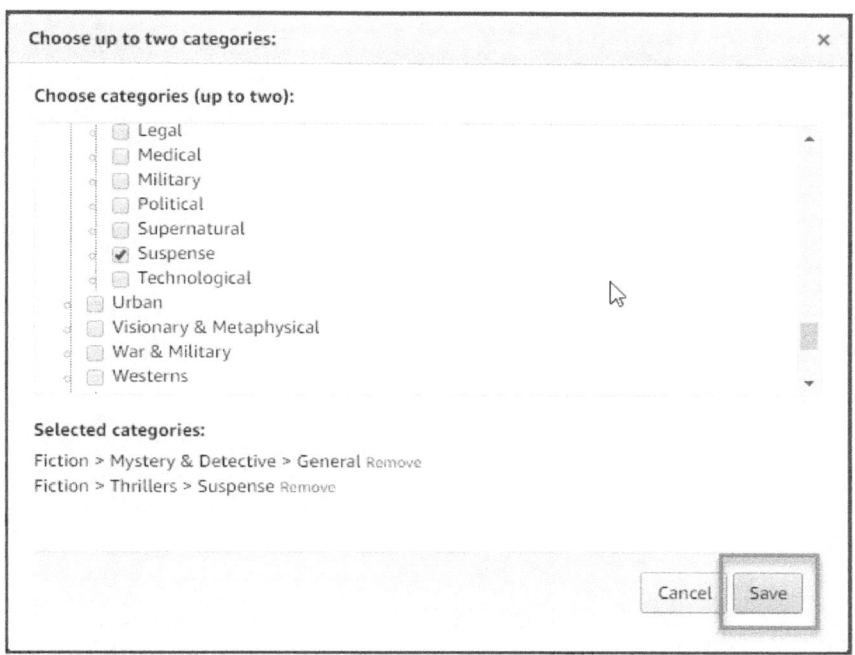

Step 8. Dance a little jig, pat yourself on the back because the hard part is over!!! *confetti

Step 9. Set your **Age and Grade range**. Specify if your book is available now or for pre-order. (More info after image.)

SELF-PUBLISHING ON A ZERO BUDGET

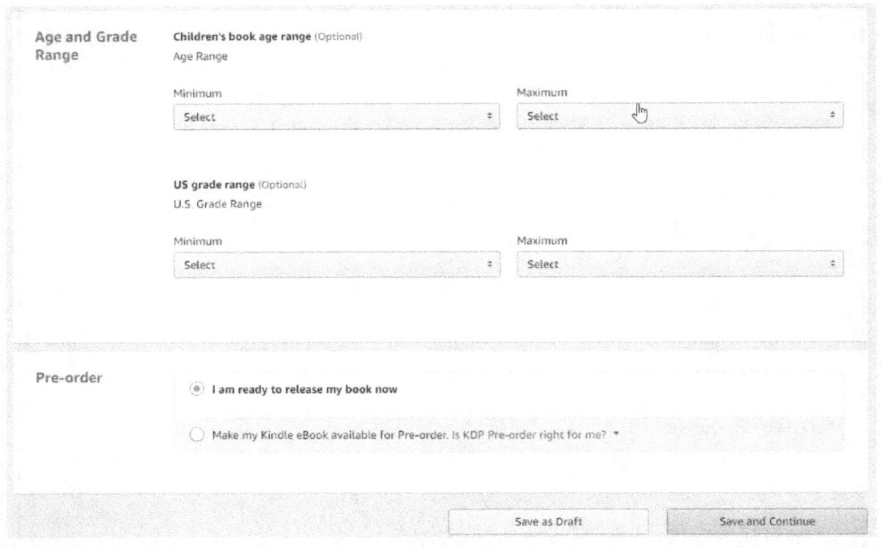

There are only two instances in which I would consider setting an Age and Grade:

- Your book is for children
- Your book is explicit (set for 18+)

Otherwise, ignore this section. Choosing specifics here can limit the distribution of your book.

Click the radio button that best specifies the availability of your book right now. In most cases this will be I am ready to release my book now.

Pre-orders are kind of an advanced feature once you've built your audience and platform.

Click **Save and Continue**.

NOTE: At this point, you can stop and come back to complete the process at a later time. Simply log into your KDP account and click your title in your **Bookshelf** to continue.

Kindle eBook Content

Congratulations! You have graduated to the next section!

In this section, we will be uploading your manuscript and cover files, so have those ready to go!

Step 1. Upload your manuscript in Word doc file format. (More info after the image.)

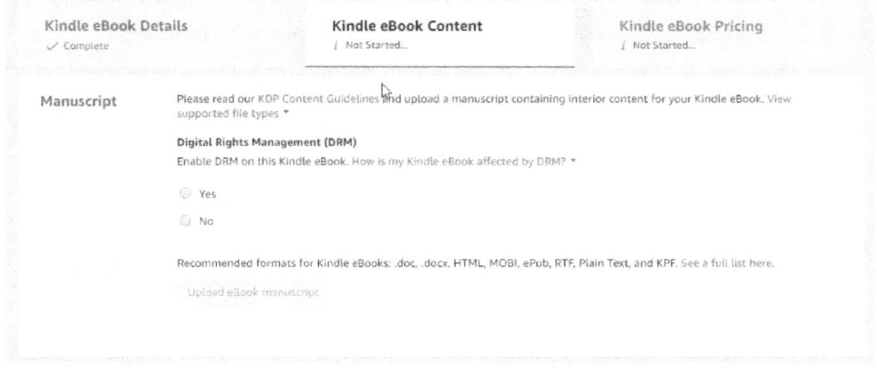

While KDP does accept multiple file types, I have found that Word is the easiest to work with because you will most likely need to make changes.

It's a lot easier just to pop over to Google Docs, make the change, and re-download a new Word file than to mess around with PDF, epub files, and other stuff in my opinion.

Just re-upload the new file and run the same checks again.

Click the radio button next to **Yes** or **No** for Digital Rights Management or DRM.

I always click **Yes** here. What DRM does is encrypt your file so it only works if it's been purchased from Amazon for a Kindle device or app. While this doesn't totally prevent piracy, it does make it more difficult.

Click the yellow **Upload eBook manuscript** button. Navigate to your file on your computer and upload it.

KDP will upload your manuscript and process the file while you continue on.

Step 2. Upload your cover file. (More info after image.)

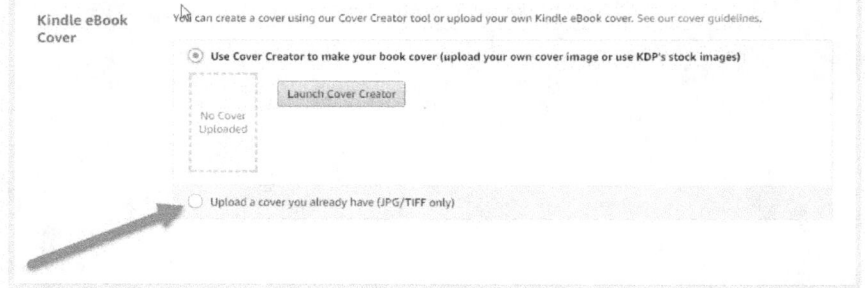

Click the radio button next to **Upload a cover you already have**.

Click the yellow **Upload** your cover file button.

KDP will upload your cover and process your file.

Step 3. Scroll back up to **Manuscript** where you previously uploaded your manuscript file and check to see if KDP found any spelling errors in your file. (More info after image.)

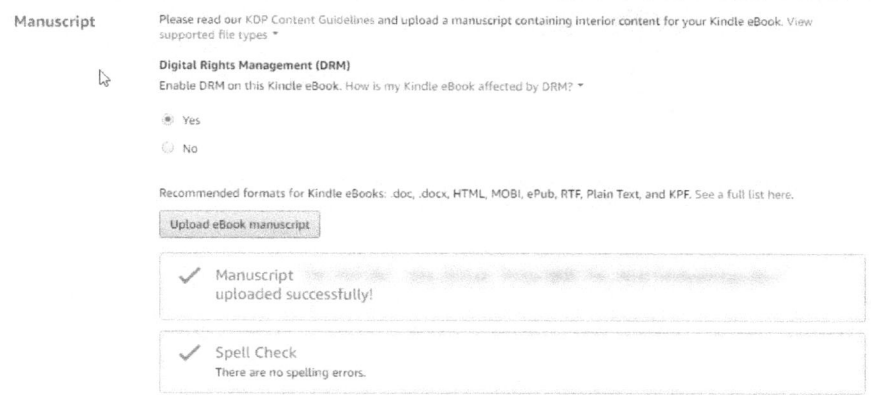

I used a dummy file here...that's why it's blurred out. You can see KDP didn't find any spelling errors. If it does, you will be able to view them here.

Then you can either fix them in your manuscript on Google Docs and re-upload a new file and/or disregard any that you need to. In the case of fiction books, made-up names and places will appear as typos here.

Scroll back down. You should notice that your cover file is uploaded, processed, and now appearing as a thumbnail in the **Kindle eBook Cover** section.

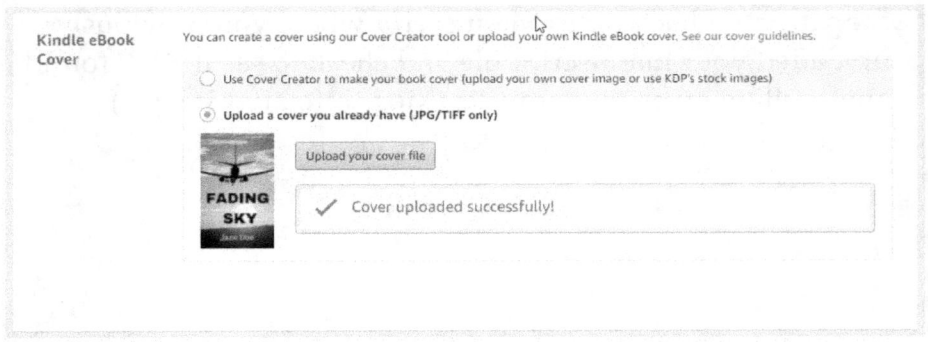

Step 4. Preview your book in the Previewer. (More info after image.)

Click the **Launch Previewer** button to take a look at how your book will look on various Kindle devices.

You can choose **Tablet**, **Phone**, or **Kindle E-reader** from the drop-down menu to view your book on a simulation of that device.

Page all the way through you book to ensure the following:

- There are Page Breaks after each heading and chapter where you wanted them
- All of your fonts fit on one line like the title, subtitle, etc.

If you see any problems, you will need to fix them in your Google Docs manuscript file, re-download your Word file, re-upload it to KDP, and check it again until you are satisfied. This process will be as easy or as painful as you make it in the formatting process covered previously.

When you are satisfied, click **Book Details** in the top-left of the Previewer screen to return to KDP.

Step 5. Type (or paste) your ISBN. Type the name of your Publisher. (More info after image.)

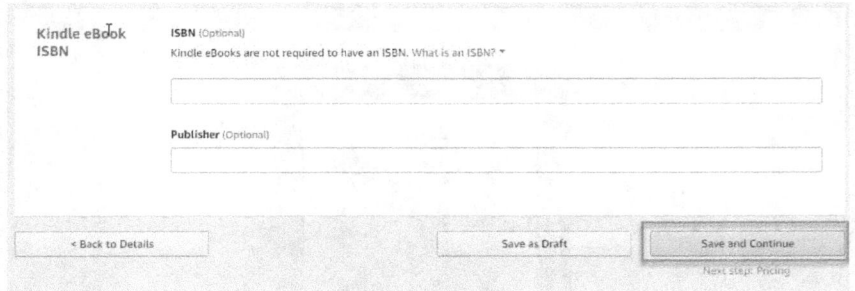

An ISBN is not required. Amazon will assign your book an AISN which is their in-house version. If you choose to publish in paperback later in this book, you can get a free ISBN then. In keeping with our ZERO budget model, I don't suggest messing with this now; however, **you can buy an ISBN if you insist**.

Type the name of your publisher. If you don't have one, use your own name, Amazon, Inc., or use a name you intend to publish all of your books under. I use my website address here.

Click **Save and Continue**.

NOTE: We've come to another point where you can take a breather if you choose. The bulk of the work is well and truly behind you. Great job!

Kindle eBook Pricing

You're nearly there!

In this section, you will figure out if you want to participate in the Kindle Select program, set a price for your book, and set your royalty amount. Oh, and you'll also decide where around the world you want your book for sale. Exciting stuff, my friends!

Step 1. Enroll your book in **Kindle Select** by clicking the checkbox if you choose. Click the radio button next to the territories where you want to sell your book. (More info after image.)

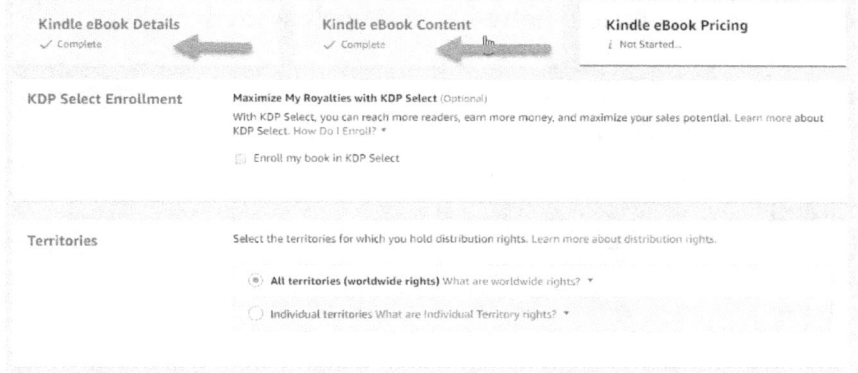

KDP Select or **Kindle Select** is a program in which you enter into a 90-day contract with Amazon. During this time, you promise exclusive digital rights to your work to Amazon only.

This does NOT include paperback and audiobook formats.

During this time you also get a few perks. You can run a promo where you can offer your book FREE for 5 days out of the entire 90. You can use this all at once or in increments. You can also do a **Kindle Countdown Deal** where your book is listed at a discount rate. See more here.

There's also some extra promotion through Amazon's various programs during this time, but it's sort of a gray area as to what the specifics are.

I do recommend **KDP Select** at least for the first 90 days just for the promotional value it provides. I usually un-enroll after that so I can distribute my book through other channels. My book stays active on Amazon of course, I just lose the ability to run promos through the **KDP Select** program.

Select your territories. I always go **Worldwide** here.

Step 2. Click the radio button next to your desired royalty amount. Select your primary marketplace from the drop-down menu and input the price for our book. (More info after image.)

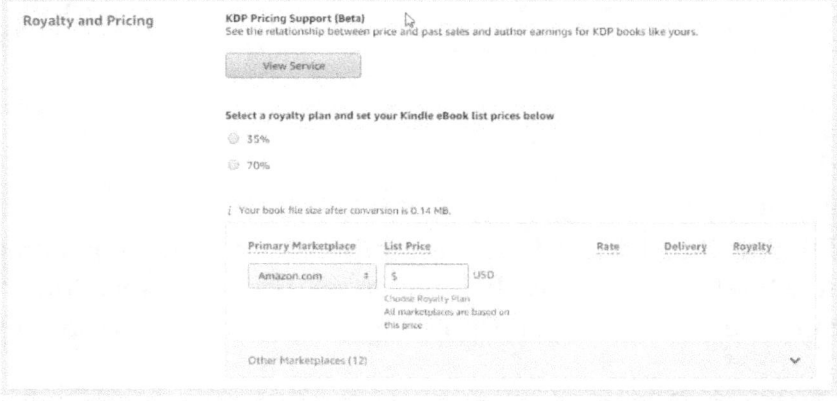

The **KDP Pricing Support** is new to me. Notice that it's in the beta testing phase. I clicked it, and it spun for 5 minutes and never produced any results. You can try your luck. I'm skipping it for now.

Choose your royalty amount by clicking the desired radio button.

This is pretty self-explanatory. 70% means you earn 70% of the purchase price of your book. 35% means you earn 35%. This is often more than traditional publishers make in royalties.

If your book is $1.99 or more, you can select the 70% royalty option. Anything under $1.99 forces you to choose 35%.

If you're not sure what to charge, you can conduct the same research we did when creating our cover to see what others in your genre are charging.

As a general rule, self-publishers are not able to charge as much as traditional publishers, but the author often makes more in royalties per sale.

A standard price for book that are less than 100 pages is $2.99. For longer works, $4.99. Most self-publishers do not venture outside of the $9.99 range.

I usually price my book in the $2.99 range. If you don't like these numbers, do your own research here.

Amazon will automatically convert your price for all 12 of its marketplaces.

The Final Step - Can You Believe It!?!

Click the check box to participate in **Kindle Matchbook** if you choose. Click the check box to allow lending if you choose to participate in **Kindle Book Lending**.

Kindle Matchbook is a program where people who buy the paperback version of your book can get a Kindle eBook copy at a discount or free. I always participate.

Kindle Book Lending is a program where you book is available for lending for up to 14 days at a time. I also participate here.

While these two options don't necessarily make me money, they do get my book further than if I didn't participate. They are also just nice gestures for your readers, and as an author now (Yay!!!), you should serve your readers whenever possible.

These are small, small ways to do that. They don't really cost you anything.

Click the **Publish Your Kindle eBook** button.

Ohmygoodness....you're done!

Now the wait begins. KDP says it can take up to 72 hours, but I've never had it take more than 24 for my book to be available. Most of the time, it's more like 12, barring weekends and holidays.

Createspace - Publishing in Paperback

Before We Get Started

Createspace is a whole different animal from KDP. To put it simply, it's clunky.

So why are we doing this to ourselves?

Let's get this discussion out of the way now. You may choose to go the KDP paperback route which would negate your need to complete this tutorial.

Createspace vs. KDP Paperback

Createspace is an Amazon-owned company, so it's seems crazy that they launched a second Print-On-Demand option.

According to Gundi Gabrielle in this article, the reason for this was simply one of visibility. Amazon added a paperback option to KDP so more people would publish in paperback as many publishers were not bothering to go through the process I share below.

I'm going to cut to the chase and examine the pro's and con's, but you can get more details from Gundi's article that I linked above ^ if you want to know more.

What Createspace has that KDP doesn't (as of this writing):

- 30-day pay out
- Canada included in U.S. distribution
- Order your book at wholesale price
- Expanded distribution to libraries, bookstores, etc.
- Ability to order a hard copy proof

Advantages of KDP Paperback:

- Combined platform for both Kindle and paperback
- Easier
- Distribution to Japan
- Keeps your older versions available during updates - Createspace pulls your book completely meaning you lose ranking and reviews, etc.

I have not published through the KDP Paperback option yet. We'll give it a try and cover it later in this series.

NOTE: Do NOT publish through both of these platforms. It will result in a dual listing on Amazon, and they'll pull both titles.

Publishing with Createspace

AVA FAILS

I happen to have a book that I need to publish, so we will go through the full process.

Step 1. Log into your Createspace account. Unlike KDP, you can't log in using your Amazon account credentials. If you don't have a Createspace account, you'll need to create one.

You will be taken to your **Dashboard**. Click the blue **Add New Title** button.

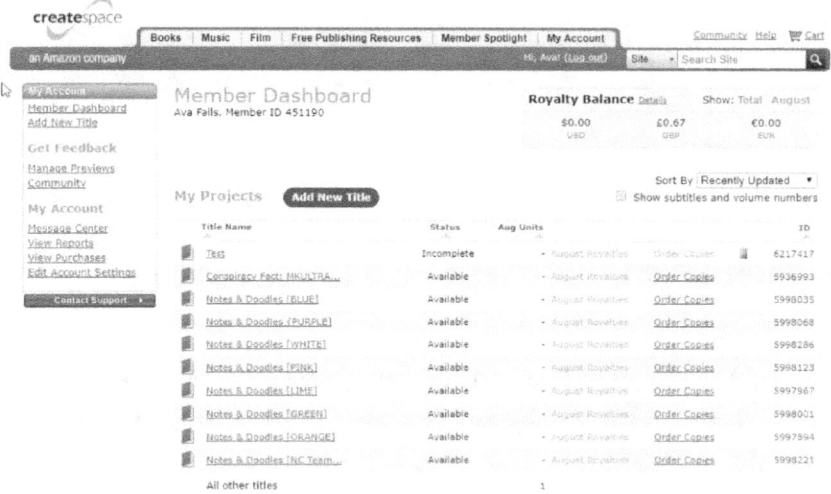

Step 2. Type the title of your book without the subtitle. Click the radio button next to **Paperback**. Click the blue **Get Started** button next to the first option: **Guided A step-by-step process with help along the way**.

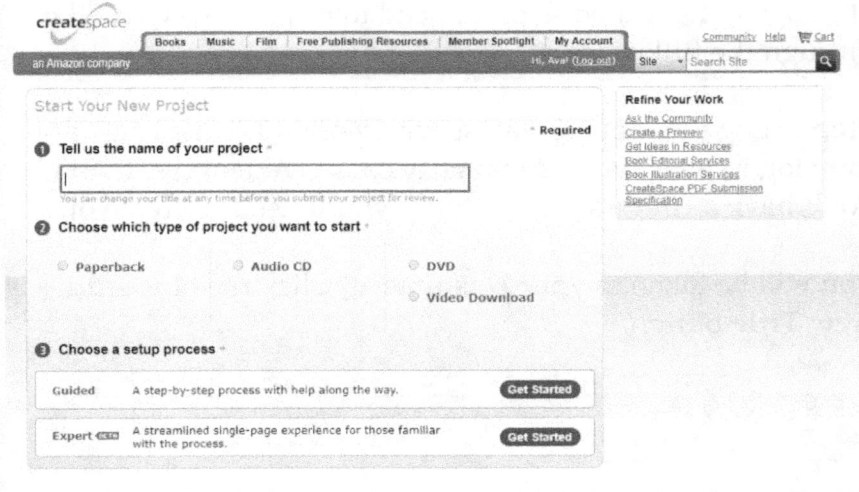

Title Information

This is the first section we will work on. Your title that you typed on the previous page will be automatically added to the **Title** field.

I'm going to put up an image of the screen, and I will run through the fields and options below.

NOTE: This information should match your Kindle book exactly so your paperback links up with your Kindle edition in the Amazon store.

AVA FAILS

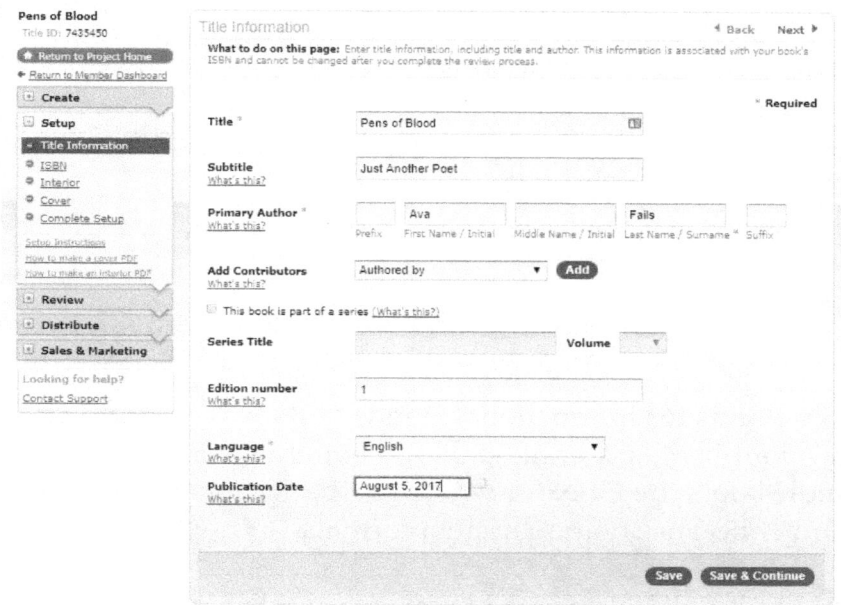

Title - Automatically populated from previous screen. If not, type your title.
Subtitle - Type your subtitle.
Primary Author - Type your name or pen name accordingly.
Add Contributors - Add any contributors to your book such as editor, illustrator, etc. If you don't have any contributors, just skip this.
Click the check box if your book is a part of a series.
Series Title and Volume - Type your Series title and volume number.
If your book isn't part of a series, skip this part.
Edition number - I always put a 1 in here in case I ever revise a book for any reason.
Language - Select the language your book is written in from the drop-down menu.
Publication Date - Type the date or click the calendar icon to the right of this field to select a date.

Click the blue **Save & Continue** button.

NOTE: None of this is set in stone. You can edit later if you need to before publishing.

ISBN

ISBN stands for International Standard Book Number. This is how your book is identified. If you bought an ISBN for your Kindle book, the ISBN for your paperback cannot be the same number because of the different formats.

You can buy ISBNs to use in your self-publishing endeavors, but they are expensive. In keeping with our ZERO budget motif, we will opt for the free one provided by Createspace.

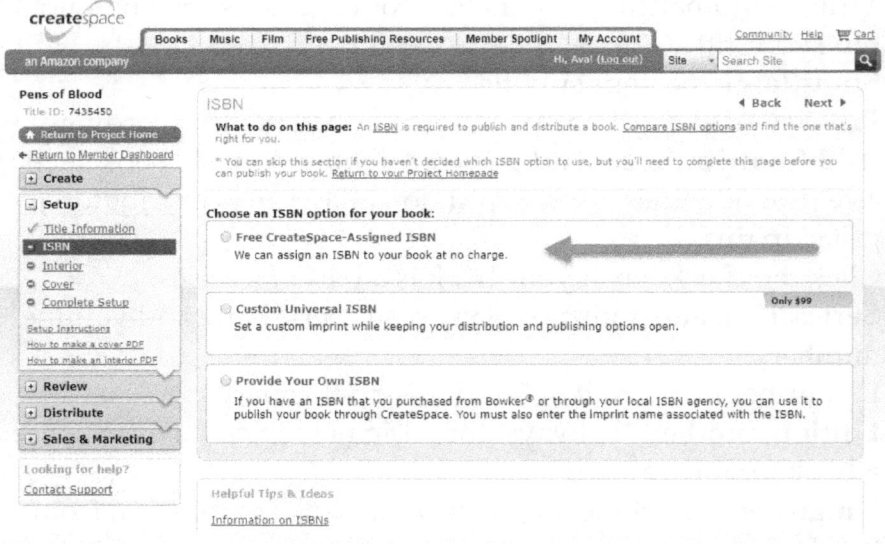

Click the radio button next to **Free CreateSpace-Assigned ISBN**.

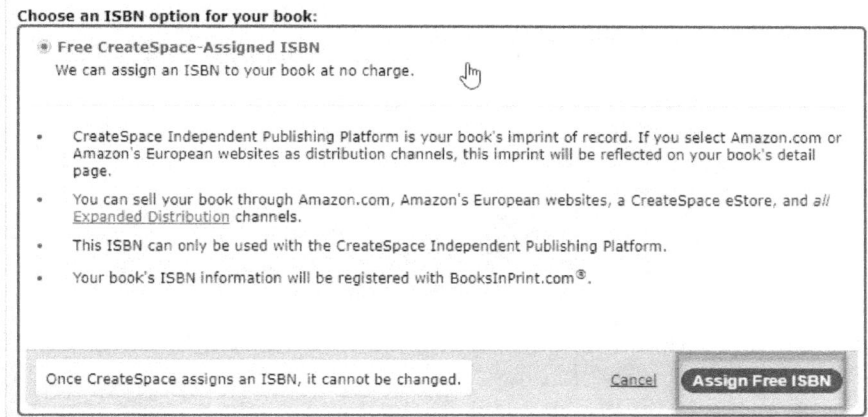

Click the blue **Assign Free ISBN** button.

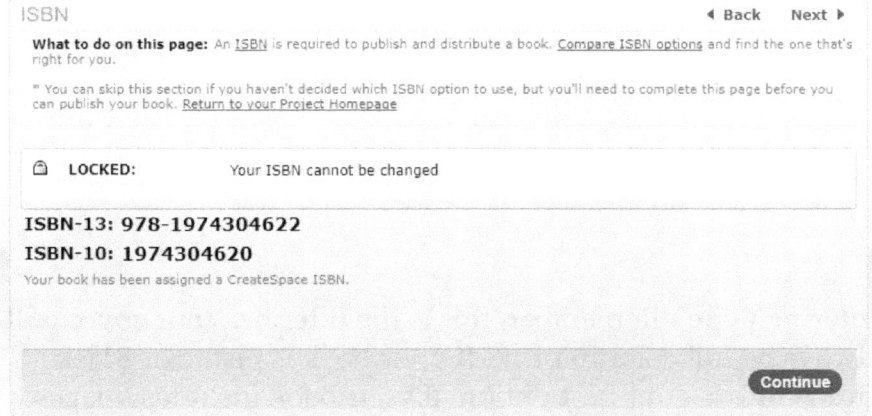

Click the blue **Continue** button.

SELF-PUBLISHING ON A ZERO BUDGET

Interior

Here's an image of the screen. I will run through everything below.

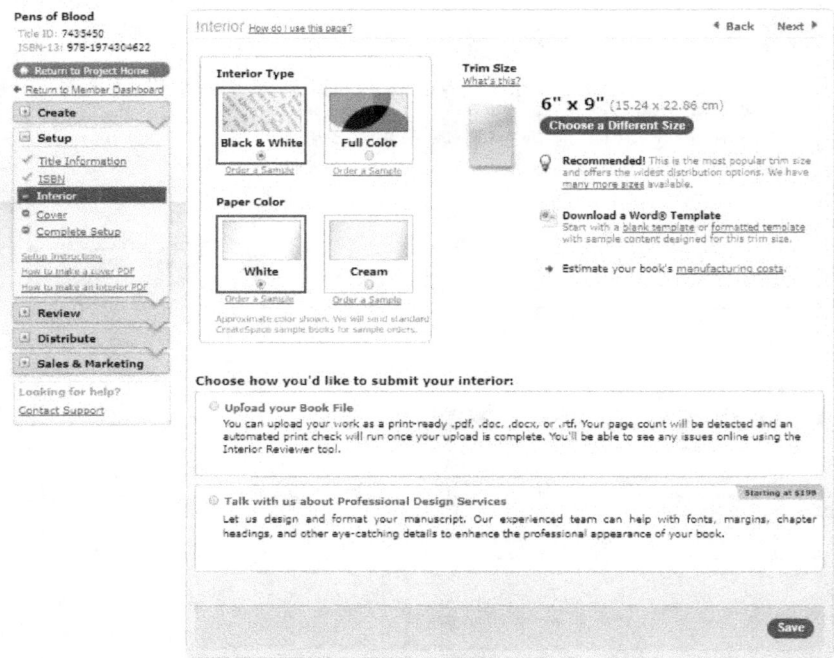

Interior Type - Remember, this is the Interior. Your cover will always be full color in print. If your book is just text, **Black and White** is your best option. If your book includes images, it's up to you to decide.

Keep in mind that your images will always appear black and white on Kindle E-reader devices like the Kindle, Paperwhite, Voyage, and Oasis.

On Fire Tablets and other Android and iOS devices with the Kindle app, the images will be color if you choose the **Full Color** option here.

Paper Color - A good general rule here is that most fiction books are on cream paper. Non-fiction, text books, or books with a lot of images tend to be printed on white paper, so choose accordingly.

Trim Size - Createspace has trim sizes ranging from 5x8 inches to 8.5x11 inches which is the size of a standard sheet of printing paper. Choosing the trim size of your book is a matter of preference really. I always go with the default 6x9 which fits in the "trade paperback" market. Check out this article for some quick help on choosing your trim size.

Choose how you'd like to submit your interior: - Click the radio button next to **Upload your Book File**.

Click the blue **Browse** button and navigate to your file on your computer.

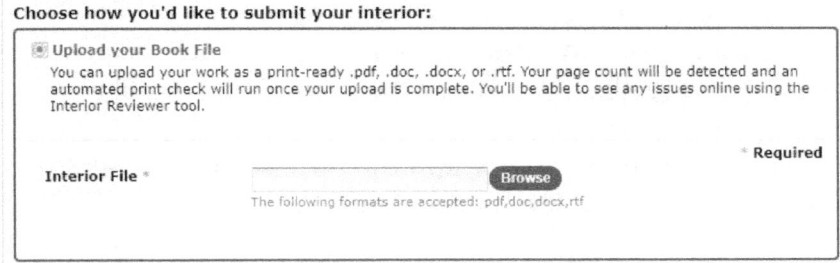

Bleed - Click the radio button under **Ends before the edge of the page** unless you are publishing a photo book.

SELF-PUBLISHING ON A ZERO BUDGET

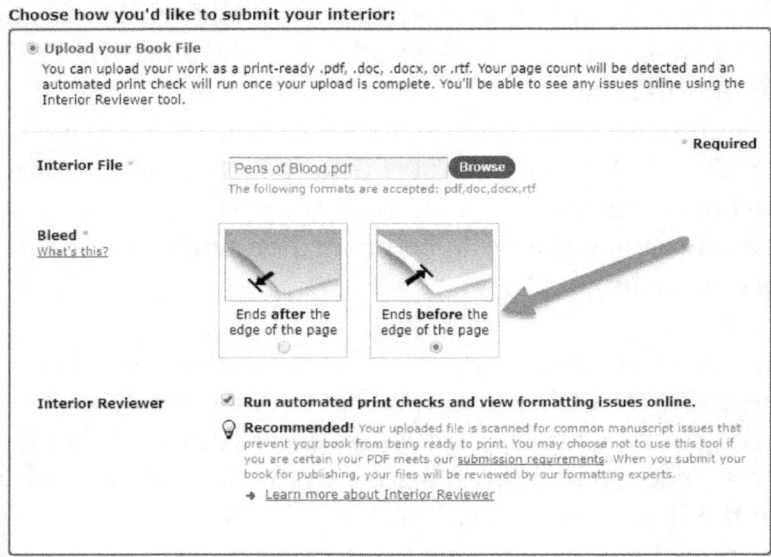

Leave the check box next to **Interior Reviewer** checked.

Click the blue **Save** button.

Createspace will upload and process your file. This may take a few minutes. You can actually start work on your cover while you wait, but we'll stay here for the sake of this tutorial.

You can navigate to any point in the publishing process by using the links in the left navigation.

AVA FAILS

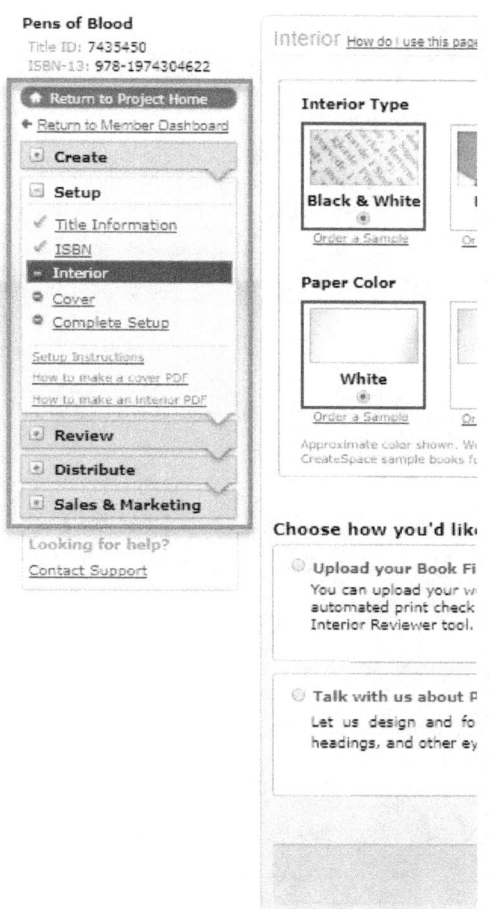

The automated print check found 8 issues with my file.

Click the blue **Launch Interior Reviewer** button to see what they are.

SELF-PUBLISHING ON A ZERO BUDGET

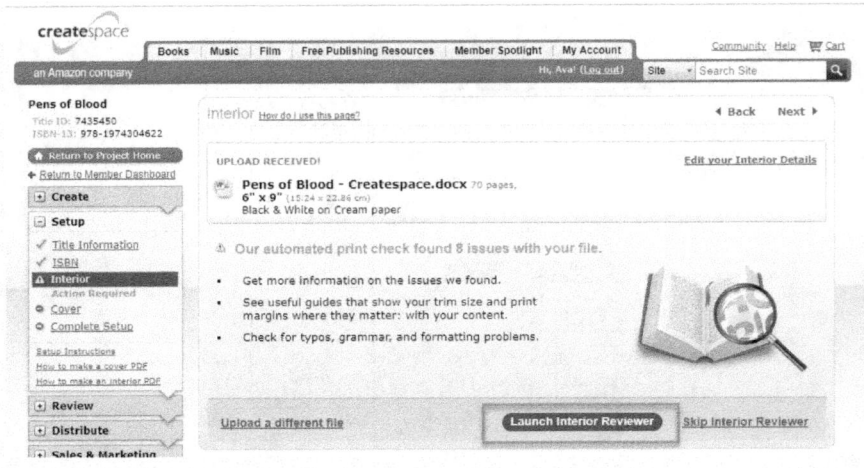

Your book will open in the Reviewer. Click **Get Started**.

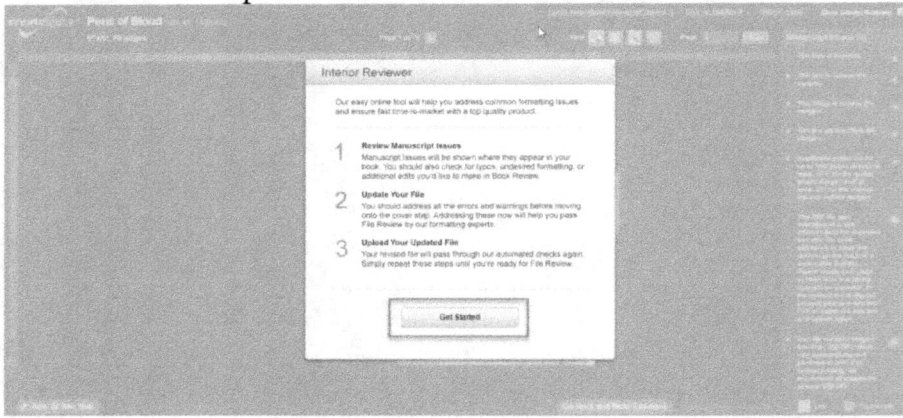

The first problem is that my book is formatted in 8.5x11. Click the button next to **Paste Into Template** to scale your pages to fit the trim size of your book.

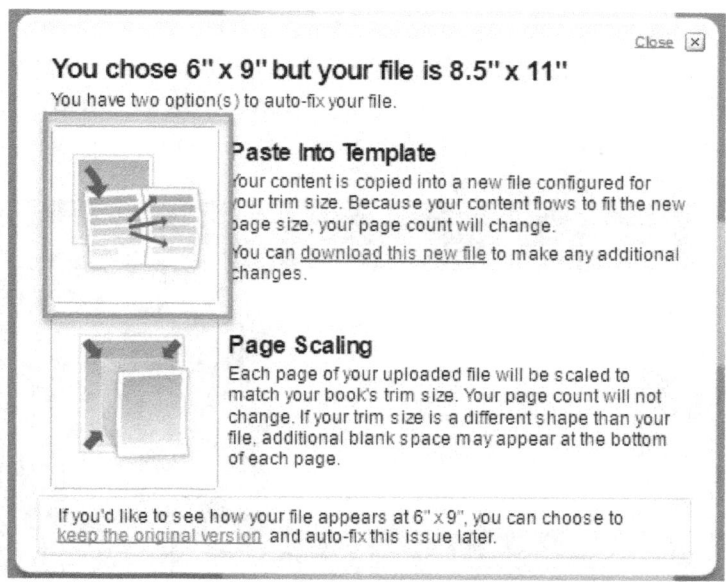

The list on the right size of the Reviewer indicates print issues with your book. Most of these probably have to do with your content being outside the trim size. The step above should fix most of them.

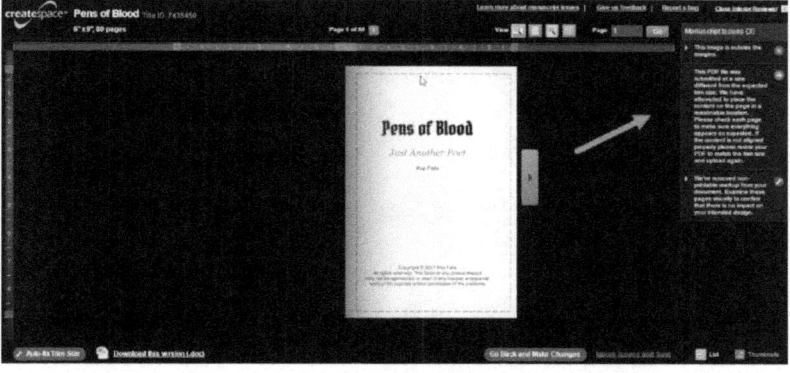

Flip through your book, using the left and right page buttons and look for formatting problems.

You will have problems, unfortunately. You may have some blank pages, or your headings and things may have moved around on the page. Click the **Download this version** link to download the newly formatted version of your file in Word doc format so you can fix it.

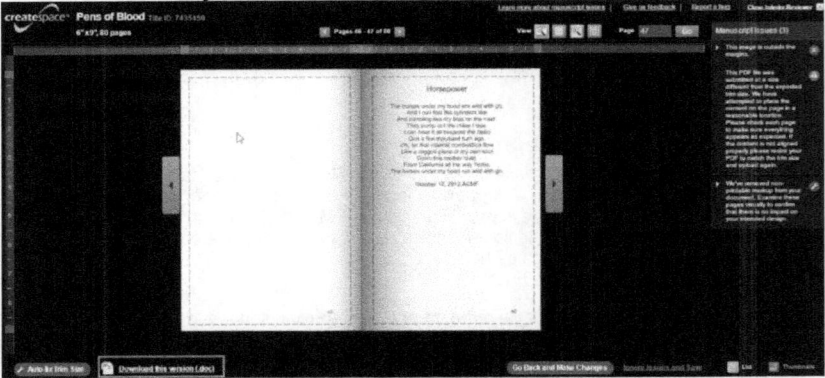

Upload the file to Google Docs by clicking the **New** button in Google Docs, then click **File upload**. Navigate to the file you downloaded from the Reviewer and upload it to Google Docs.

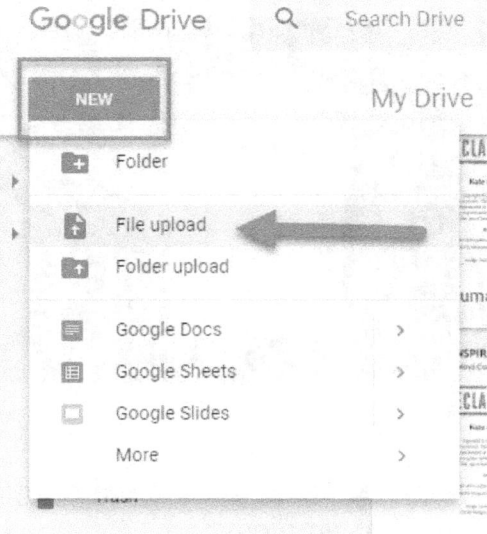

Right-click the uploaded file in your Google Drive, hover your cursor over **Open with**, and select **Google Docs** from the fly-out menu to open it.

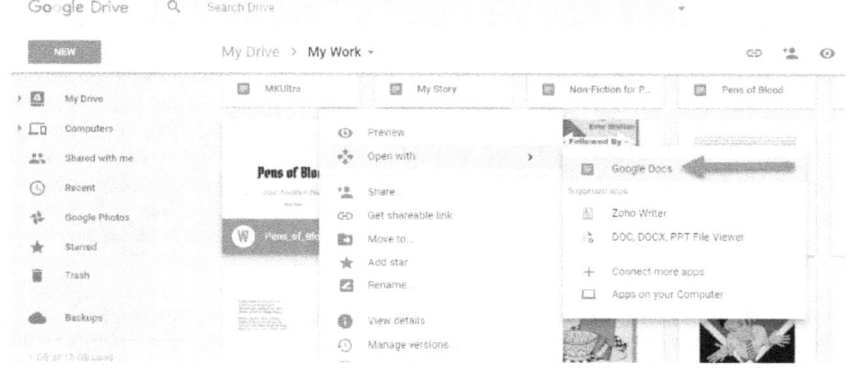

Go through your file and make the necessary changes. Re-download it as a Word file. Delete the old one.

Go back to Createspace.

Click the **Go Back and Make Changes** button in the Reviewer.

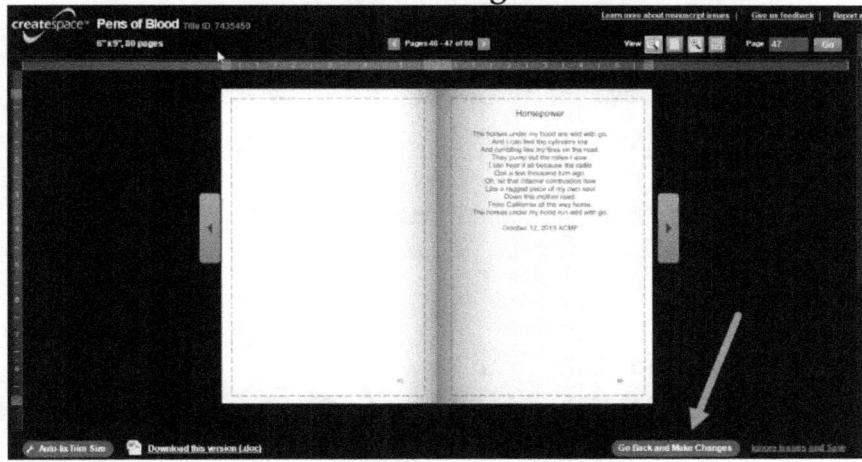

SELF-PUBLISHING ON A ZERO BUDGET

Click the **Upload a different file** link.

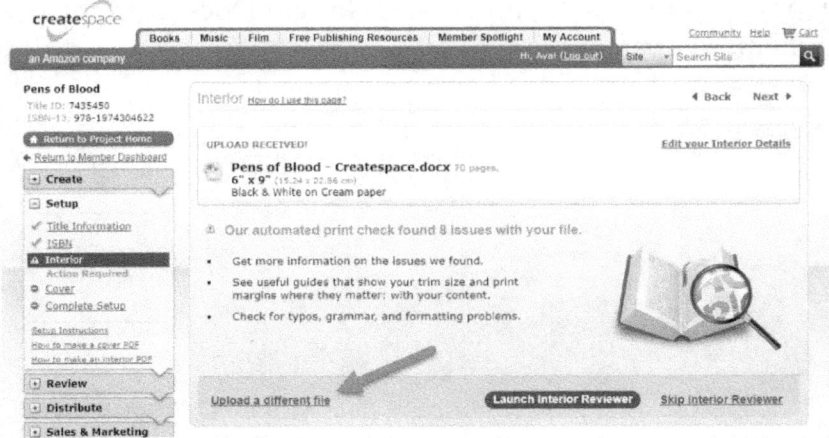

Click the **Upload a different file** link.

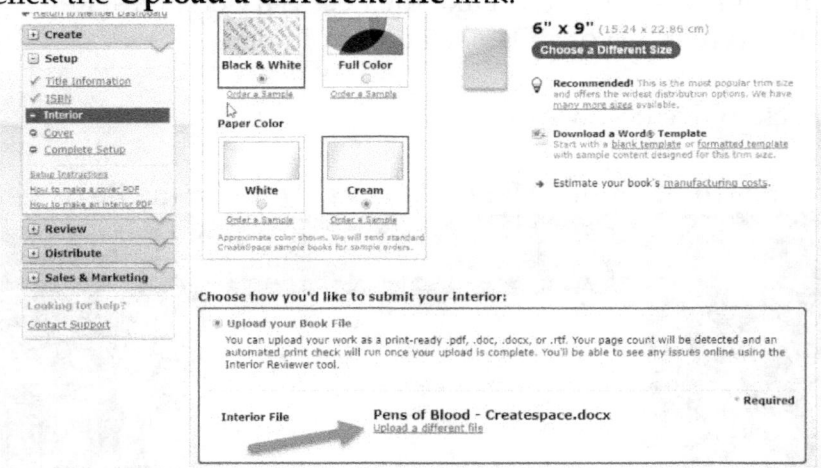

Click **Browse** and select your new file.

Click **Save**.

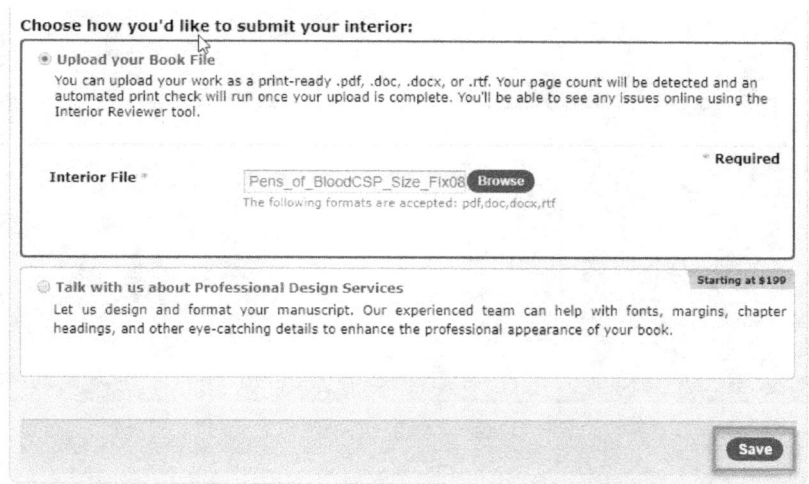

Deja vu? Yeah. This is the aforementioned clunky part.

Createspace will upload, process your file, and assess it for errors...again.

It should have significantly fewer issues this time.

Launch the Interior Reviewer again.

Page through and make sure everything looks good. You can see I have no more issues. The Reviewer is telling me to the right that it resized my pages to fit. If all looks good, click the blue **Save and Continue** button.

SELF-PUBLISHING ON A ZERO BUDGET

You will be returned to the previous screen. It will probably still indicate 1 issue which is simply referring to the aforementioned page resizing.

Take note of how many pages are in your book. You will need this information for your cover template.

Click the blue **Ignore Issues and Continue** button.

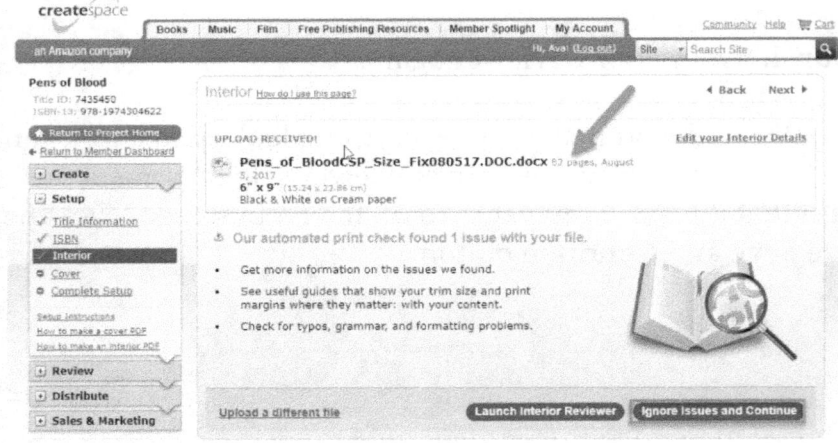

Cover

1. Select a finish for your book cover: - This is a matter of preference. Click the radio button under **Matte** or **Glossy**.

2. Choose how to submit the cover of your book:

Click the radio button next to **Upload a Print-Ready PDF Cover**.

Go here -
https://www.createspace.com/Help/Book/Artwork.do
Fill in the details for your book. Don't necessarily copy those below. They are mine.

Click the **Build Template** button.

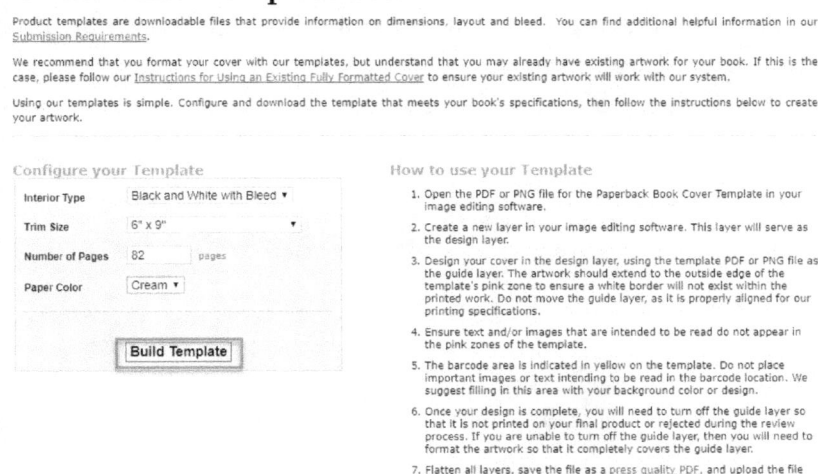

Click the link to download the zip file with your template inside.

SELF-PUBLISHING ON A ZERO BUDGET

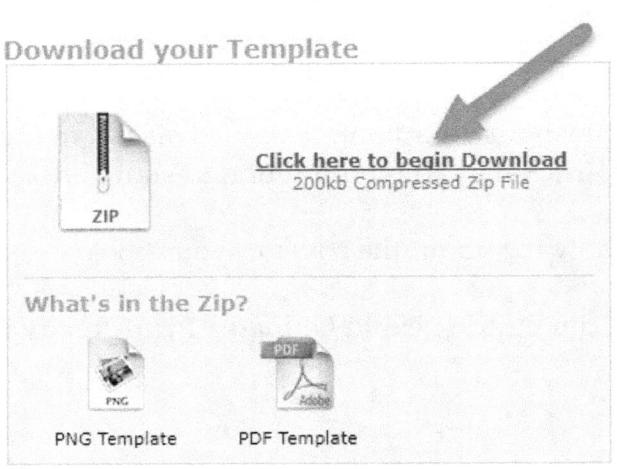

Unzip the template.
Go to https://www.sumopaint.com/home/. We are using this because it's free, online, and something most people can use; however, if you are proficient in Photoshop, Gimp, or another program, feel free to use it.
Click the big gray **Try Online** button.

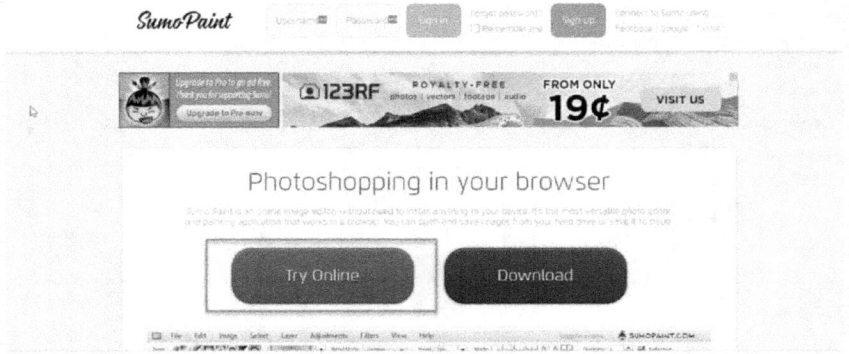

Click **File** and click **Open from My Computer** in the drop-down menu.

AVA FAILS

Navigate to the PNG file of your cover template inside your unzipped folder and open it. Your cover template will open in SumoPaint.

Go ahead and click the **Move Tool** in **Tools**.

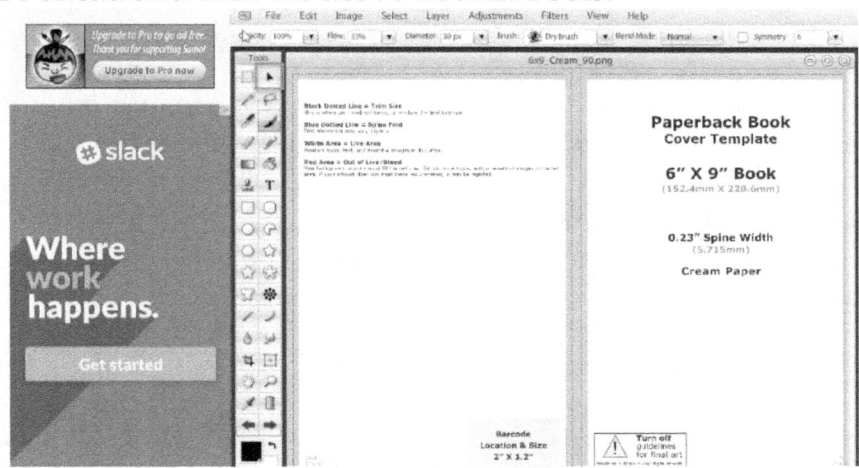

Click **File**, hover your cursor over **Import to Layer**, and click **From My Computer** in the fly-out menu.

Navigate to your Kindle cover file on your computer and import it into SumoPaint.

SumoPaint will import your Kindle cover.

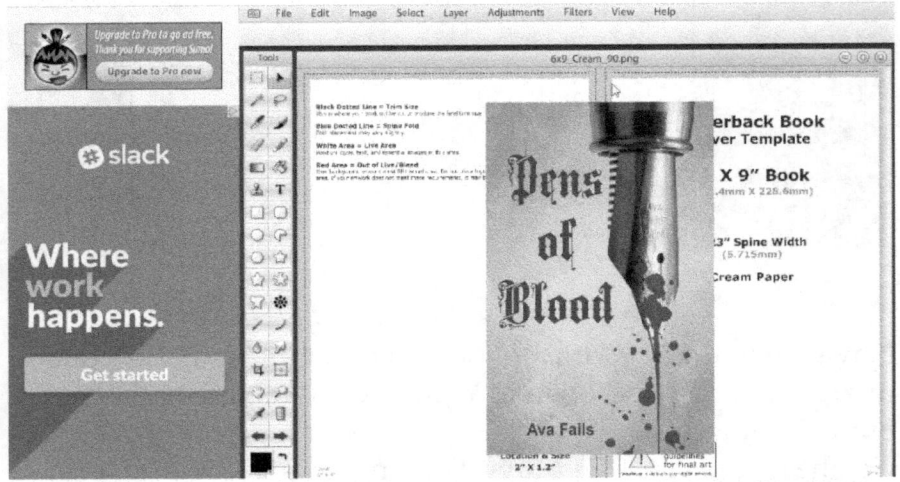

Move your cover to the general vicinity it belongs in. You will need to make sure the layer that item is on is selected when you are working with it in the Layers menu in the right sidebar. If you can't move something, its Layer probably isn't selected. If the Layers are off-screen, click the arrows to shorten the other items like the Advertisement.

With your cover layer selected, right-click and select **Free Transform** from the menu.

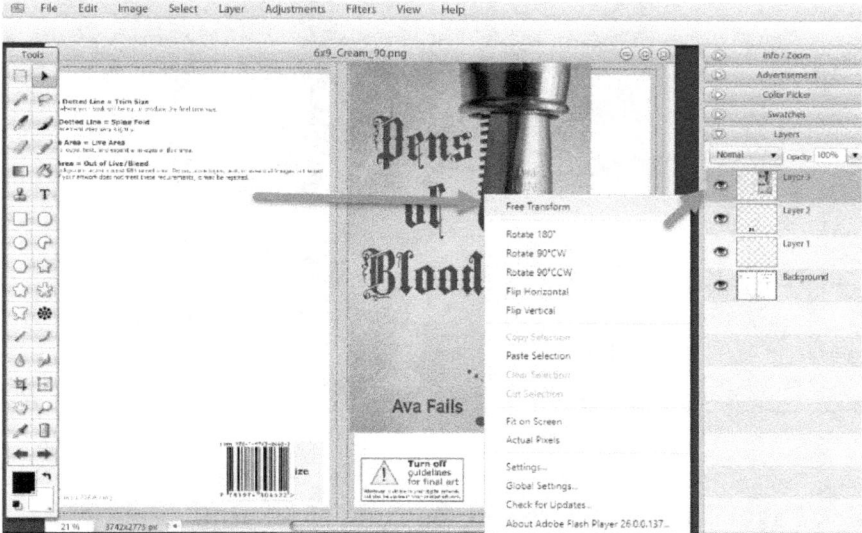

Resize the cover image to fill the right side of your template which makes up the front cover of your book up to the dotted line that indicates the spine.

Fit the image all the way to the edges as shown.

When you're done, click the **Move Tool** to deselect the image.

SELF-PUBLISHING ON A ZERO BUDGET

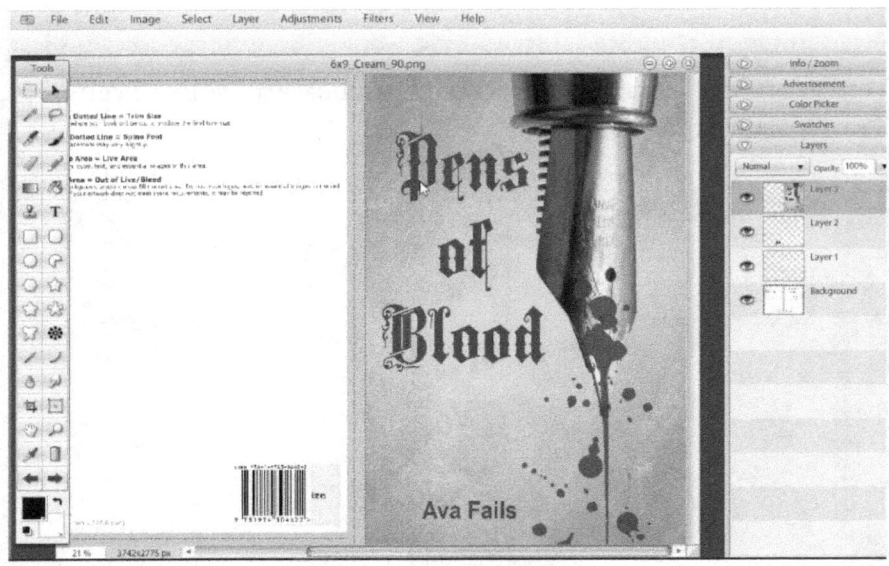

Click **Layer 1** under **Layers** in the right sidebar. If there isn't a Layer 1, create one by clicking **Layer** and select **Add New Layer** from the drop-down menu.

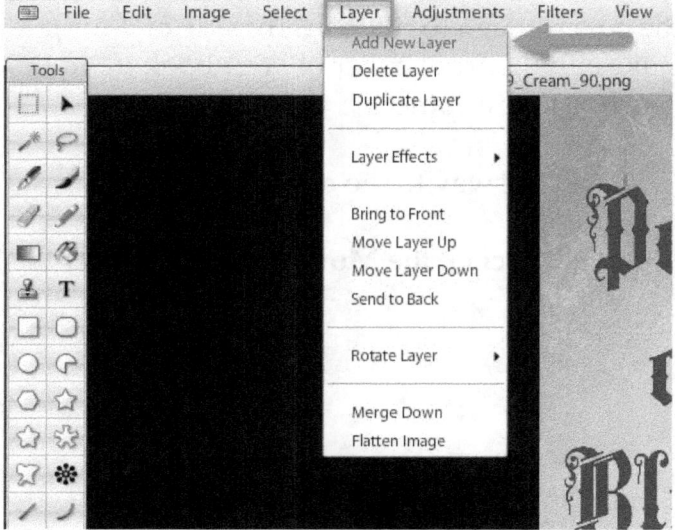

Drag and drop the new layer so it is between the Background and your barcode under Layers in the right sidebar.

Click the **Paint Bucket Tool** under Tools. The colored square at the bottom indicates the color. Black works fine for me, but I'll show you how to change it below.

SIDENOTE: As with KDP, you can Save, come back to this any time, and pick up where you left off. Take breaks as needed!

To choose a different color, click the **Eyedropper Tool** under **Tools** and click any color on your front cover to match it. It will be indicated in the **Foreground Color** square below.

SELF-PUBLISHING ON A ZERO BUDGET

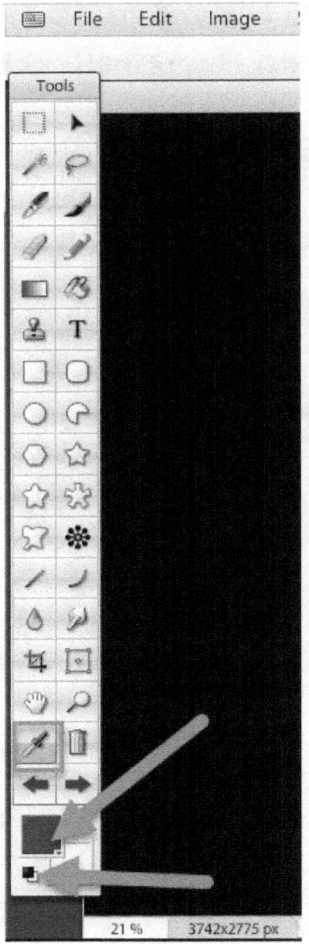

If you need to return to the Black/White squares, simply click the icon below the **Foreground Color** as indicated.

NOTE: You can use SumoPaint in full screen mode if you are having trouble with tools or your cover being offscreen. Click **View**, hover your cursor over **Screen Mode**, and select **Full Screen Mode** from the fly-out menu.

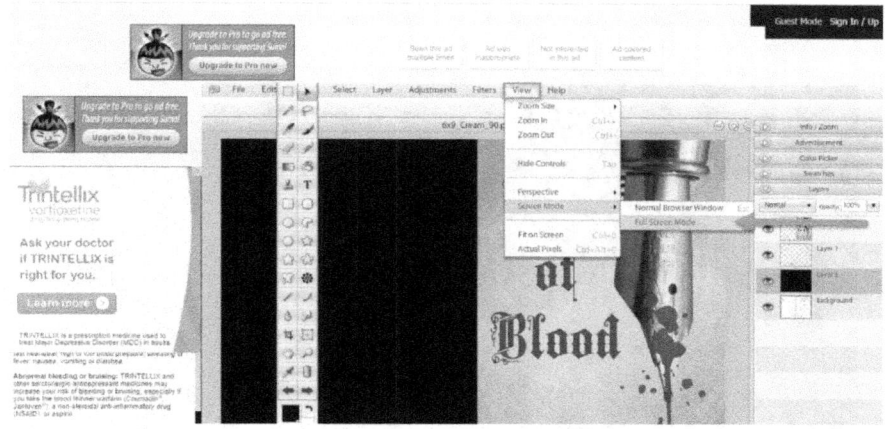

NOTE: You can view the Background layer (your template) by clicking the Eye icon next to that layer to check your placement.

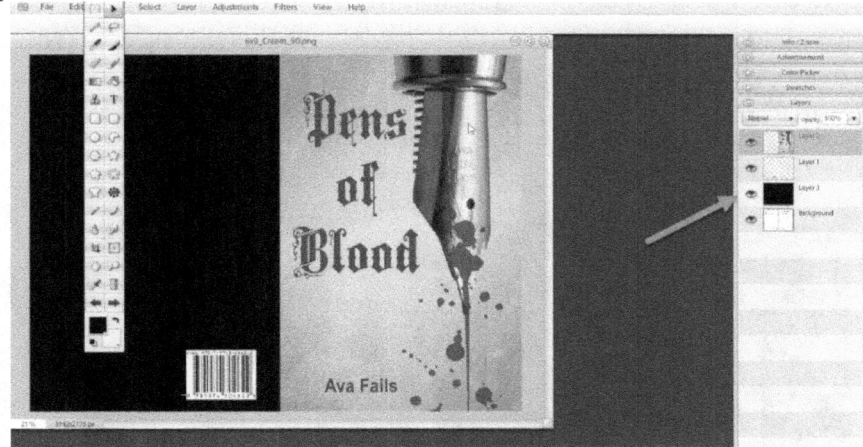

Add a new layer.
With the new layer selected in the right sidebar, click the **Text Tool**.

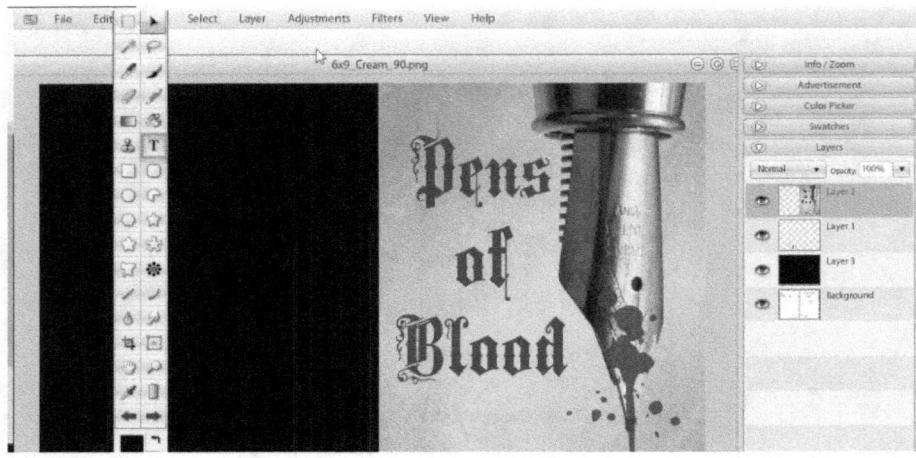

I usually just copy and paste my description here. Yes, the same one I used when I uploaded my Kindle version. As you know the back cover is simply for your book's synopsis. You can put whatever you want here. Format your text and color it using the tools provided at the top of the SumoPaint screen.

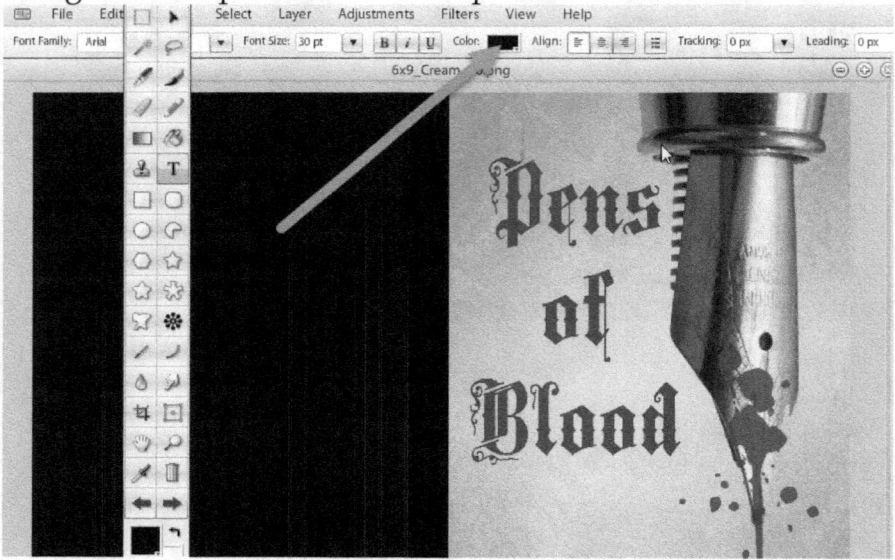

My spine is too thin to add my title and author there, but yours may not be.

Add a new text layer the same way you did above and type your Title and Author. Click **Layer**, hover your cursor over **Rotate Layer** and select **Rotate 90 CW**.

Click the **Move Tool** and place this on your spine accordingly. Once you are happy with your cover, click **File**, and then click **Save to My Computer...**

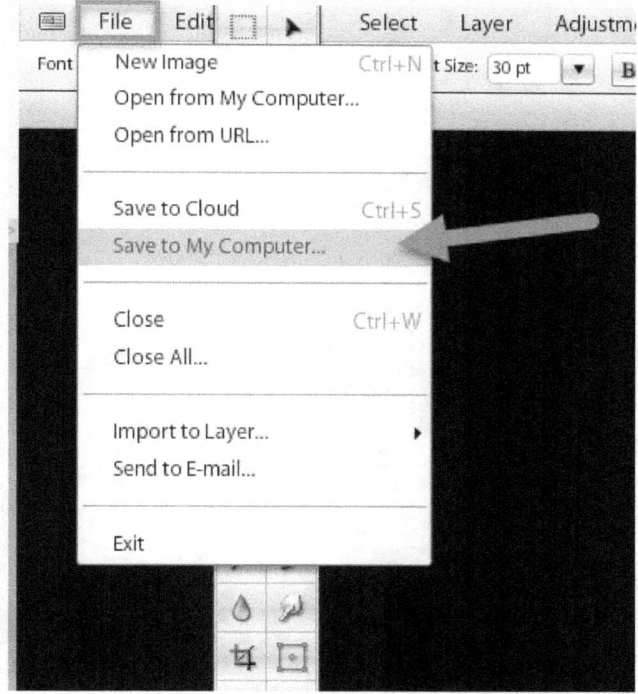

Your Createspace cover will be saved to your computer.

Go to http://png2pdf.com/
Upload your cover image PNG file. This will take a minute or so.

Click the yellow **Download** button to download your cover as a PDF.

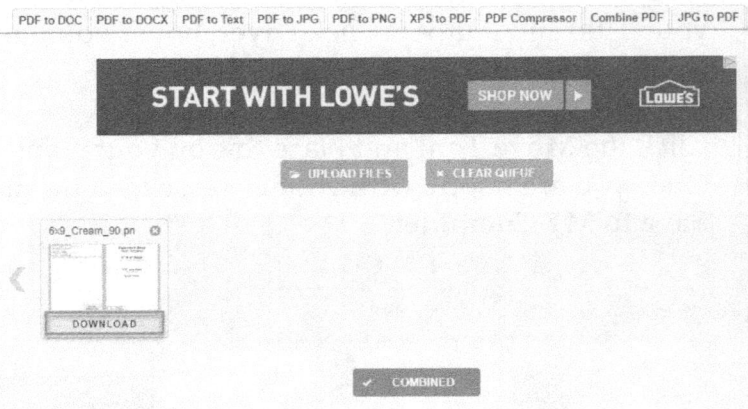

FINALLY!
Here's what my cover ended up looking like:

Go back to Createspace.

Navigate to your cover file on your computer by clicking **Browse**.

Click **Save**.

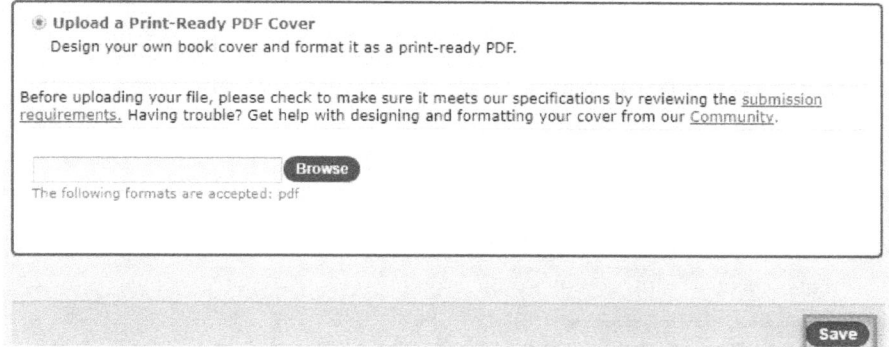

This will take a minute or so.

All done. Click the blue **Continue** button.

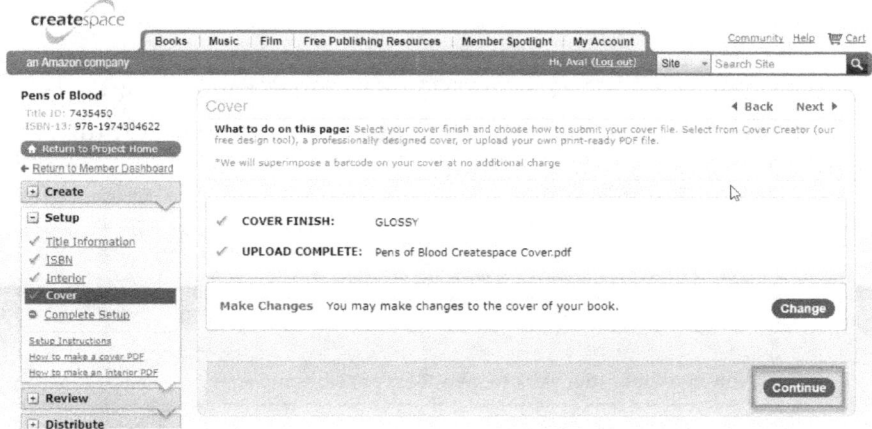

Complete Setup

SELF-PUBLISHING ON A ZERO BUDGET

Confirm that your book title, ISBN, book files and other elements are correct.

Review the Member Agreement.

Once you're satisfied with everything, click the blue **Submit Files for Review** button.

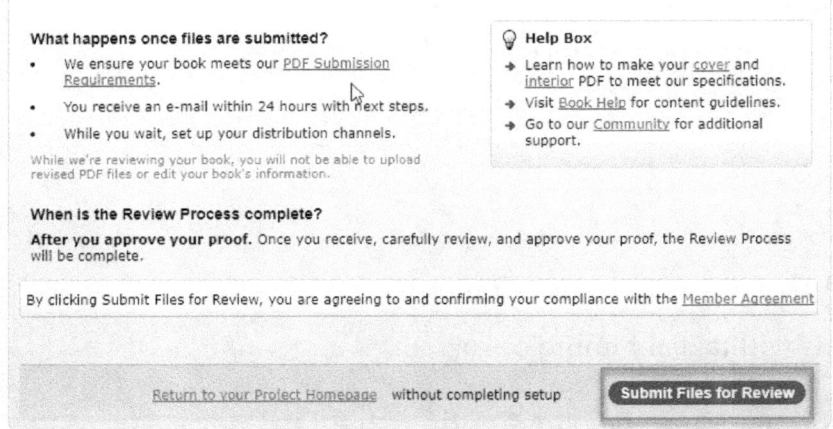

Createspace will review your files to ensure they meet their requirements and are printable. You will receive an email within 24 hours. Click **Continue**.

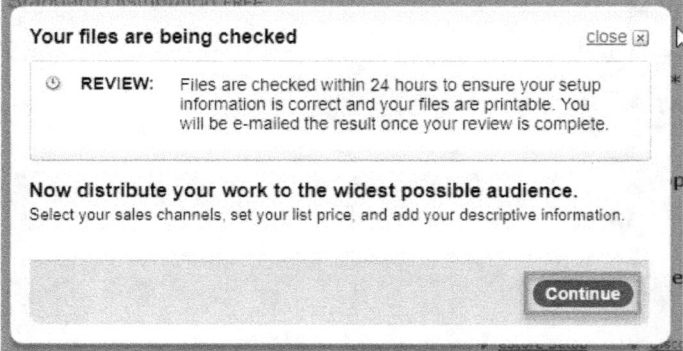

Channels

This is where you specify where and how you want your paperback book distributed. Standard Distribution includes the following which are all selected by default:

- Amazon.com
- Amazon Europe
- CreateSpace eStore

If for some reason, you don't want to distribute to one or more of these, simply click the blue arrow(s) to deselect that channel.

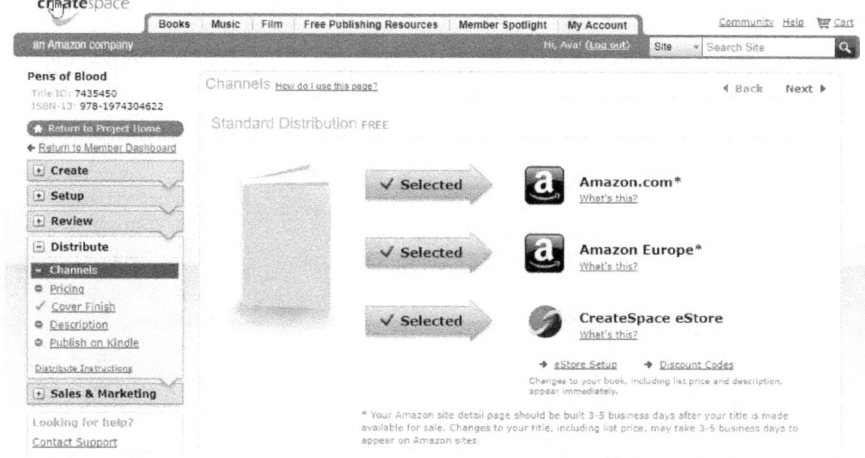

Under **Expanded Distribution**, you will notice that **Bookstore and Online Retailers** is grayed out. Click to select your BISAC code to make this channel available.

SELF-PUBLISHING ON A ZERO BUDGET

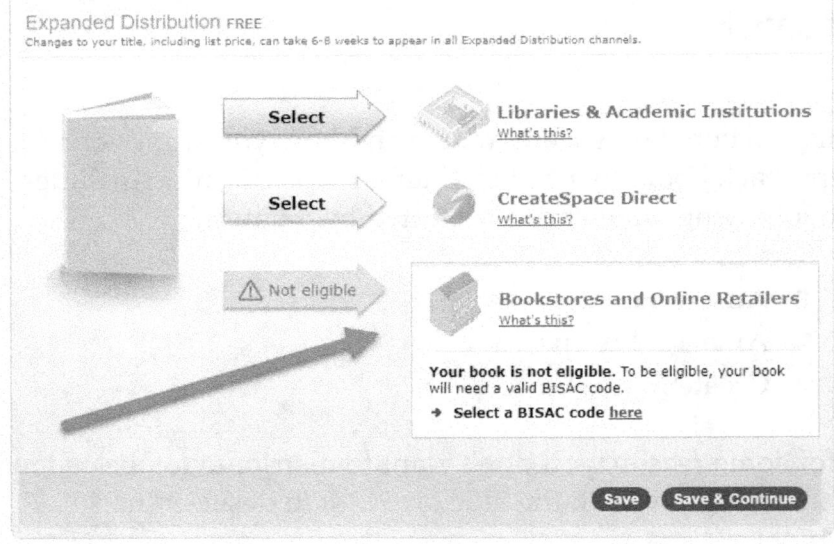

I'm going share the image and then discuss what to do below:

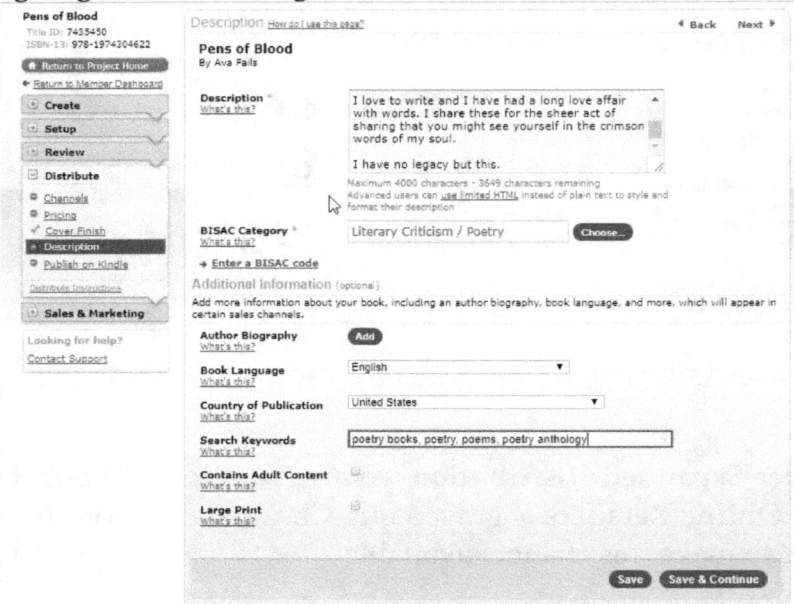

Description - Copy and paste your description. It's fine to use the same one from when you published your Kindle book in KDP.

BISAC Category - You can only select one, so select the most specific one that matches the ones you chose for your Kindle book by clicking the blue **Choose** button.

Author Biography - Add this by clicking the blue **Add** button.

Book Language - Select the language your book is written in from the drop-down menu.

Country of Publication - Select the country of publication from the drop-down menu.

Search Keywords - Type your keywords. These can be the same ones you used for your Kindle book.

Contains Adult Content - Check this is your book contains adult content. If not, leave unchecked.

Large Print - Check this if your book is in large print. If not, leave unchecked.

Click **Save**.

Click **Channels** in the left navigation. You will now be able to select your desired channels under **Expanded Distribution**. Once you're done, click **Save and Continue**.

Pricing

Last step!

You will notice that Createspace gives you a minimum list price. You will need to charge at least this amount, but preferably more to profit from your book.

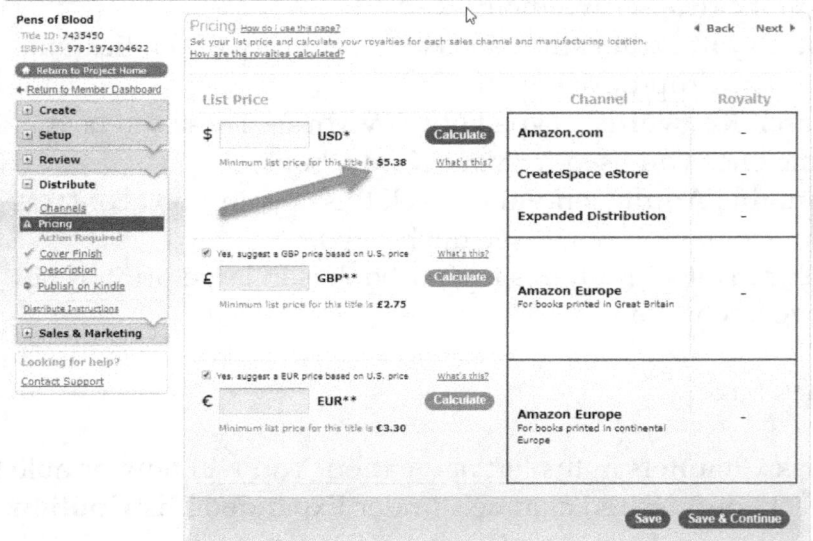

Type your price and click the blue **Calculate** button. Createspace will calculate your royalty and also convert the other prices on the page for you.

Click **Save and Continue**.

You are done for now. If Createspace prompts you to publish to KDP, simply click out of the screen since we already published our book for Kindle.

Now it's a waiting game. Wait for your email from Createspace. Once you receive it and there aren't any changes to be made, you can order a print proof of your book to look it over for a few bucks or approve a digital proof for print.

After you approve your proof, your book will be available through the distribution channels you select. You should allow about 5 business days for it to begin showing up alongside your Kindle edition in the Amazon store.

CONGRATULATIONS!

Those paperbacks make awesome gifts!

Paperback! You're amazing. Your friends and family are going to love seeing you on their bookshelves.

Managing Your Royalties

Let's get paid!

You have gone through the hard work of writing, editing, formatting, and publishing your own book. It's a fantastic feeling, isn't it?!

Let's make sure you are set up to receive your royalty payments from your hard work.

You will wait 60 long days for your first payments from Amazon for you Kindle books. Createspace pays out every 30 days. After you publish your first book, if it sells consistently, you should see payments each month following that first, long 60 days.

I started my own self-publishing journey in 2011, and I've received royalty payments for my efforts every month since.

Getting Paid from Kindle Direct Publishing (KDP)

Step 1. Log into your KDP account. Navigate to your **Bookshelf** if it doesn't default there.

Step 2. Click on your account name at the top of your screen.

AVA FAILS

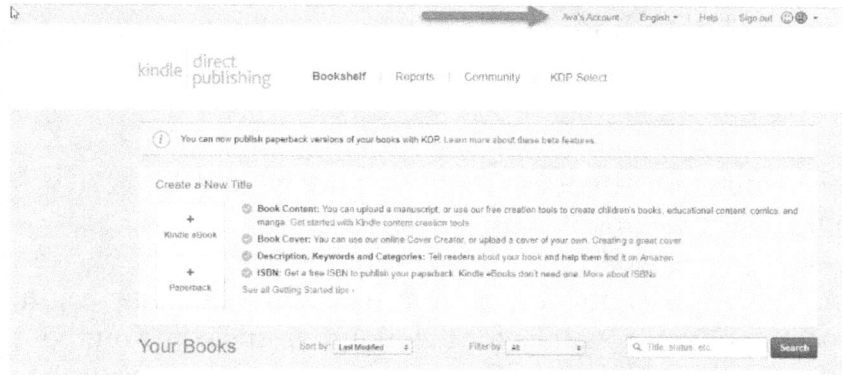

Step 3. Scroll down to **Payment & Banking** and input your banking information. You need a routing and account number.

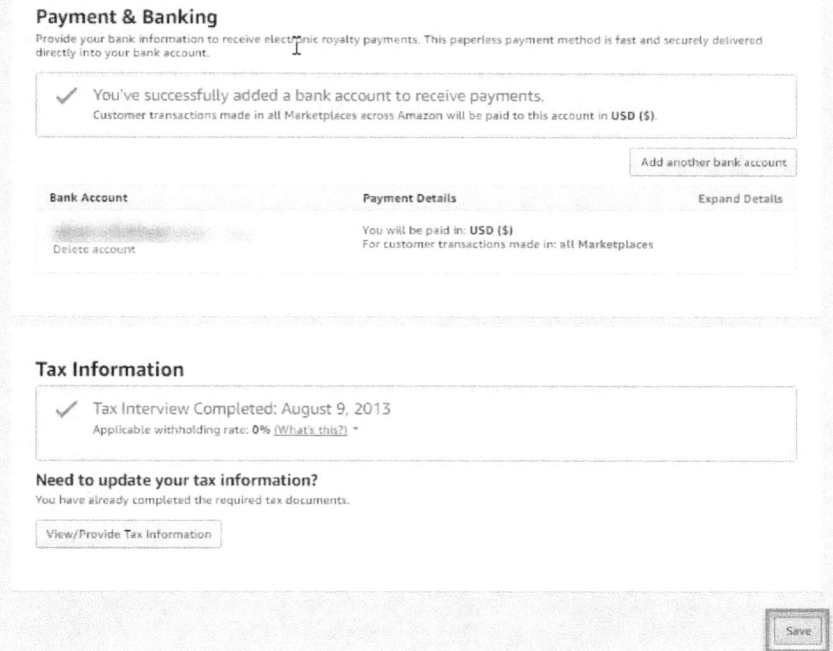

Step 4. Fill out your tax information accordingly. This is usually just a W-9. This form is a W-8 for peoples outside the United States.

Once your complete these steps, you are eligible to receive your royalty payments.

You'll receive several emails from Amazon when they begin processing your royalties for the month. Mine come on the 20th of each month. Payments appear in my bank account on the 29th.

Checking Your Royalty Reports in KDP

Step 1. From your **Account Settings** click **Reports**. If you're back in your **Bookshelf**, also click **Reports** in the top navigation.

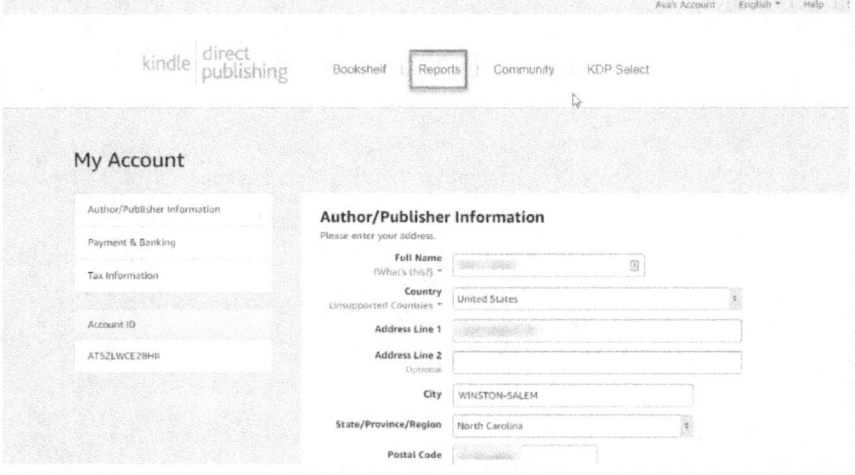

From this page you can view bar graphs of your current sales and your KENP.

Wait, what the heck is KENP?

This stands for Kindle Edition Normalized Pages. This is the number of pages read in your books from those who have Kindle Unlimited or have borrowed them through the Kindle Owner's Lending Library (KOLL).

You won't get rich from this since the current payout is just under 1/2 cent per page read.

We talked about this during the KDP publishing process. If you didn't choose the lending option during publishing, you can disregard KENP for the most part.

Step 2. Check out your current royalties by scrolling a little further down the page. You can generate a report from here for your records if you wish.

Royalties Earned (What's this?)

Marketplace	Currency	eBook Royalty	Paperback Royalty	Total Royalty
Amazon.com	USD			
Amazon.co.uk	GBP			
Amazon.de	EUR			
Amazon.fr	EUR			
Amazon.es	EUR			
Amazon.it	EUR			
Amazon.nl	EUR			
Amazon.co.jp	JPY			
Amazon.in	INR			
Amazon.ca	CAD			
Amazon.com.br	BRL			
Amazon.com.mx	MXN			
Amazon.com.au	AUD			

Generate Report (What's this?)

My favorite report is the **Month-to-Date** report. Scroll up and check out the tabs at the top. These display various information regarding your sales. The **Month-to-Date** report shows all your sales for the current month.

AVA FAILS

Click around and explore on your own. The **Prior Months' Royalties** will allow you download Excel files of your royalties for your records.

NOTE: If you need support or want to know more about any part of KDP, click the **Community** tab in the top navigation.

Getting Paid from Createspace

Step 1. Log into your Createspace account. Click **Edit Account Settings** in the left navigation.

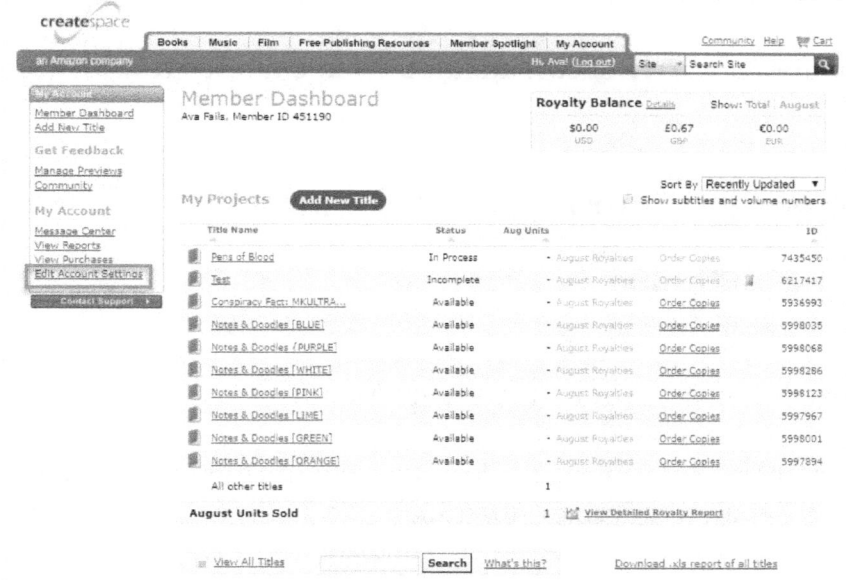

Step 2. Click the link under **Royalty Payment Information**.

SELF-PUBLISHING ON A ZERO BUDGET

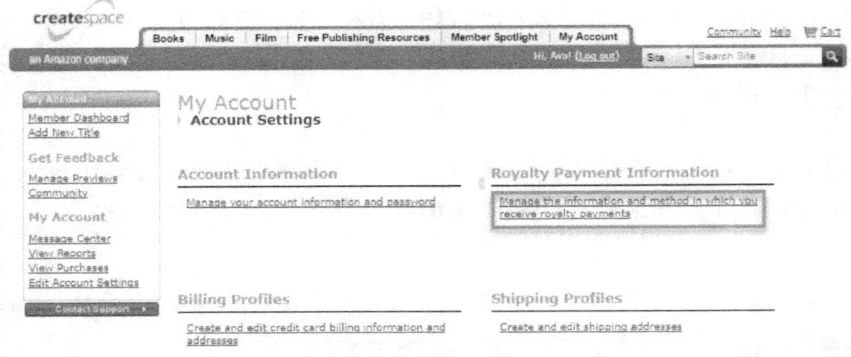

Click the blue **Edit** button to add your banking account information and then fill out your tax information. This will be pretty much the same process you followed for KDP.

Createspace pays once a month the same time as KDP.

Checking Your Royalty Reports in Createspace

Step 1. Log into your Createspace Member Dashboard.

From here you can see a brief overview of your current sales, see a detailed report, or download Excel files for your records.

AVA FAILS

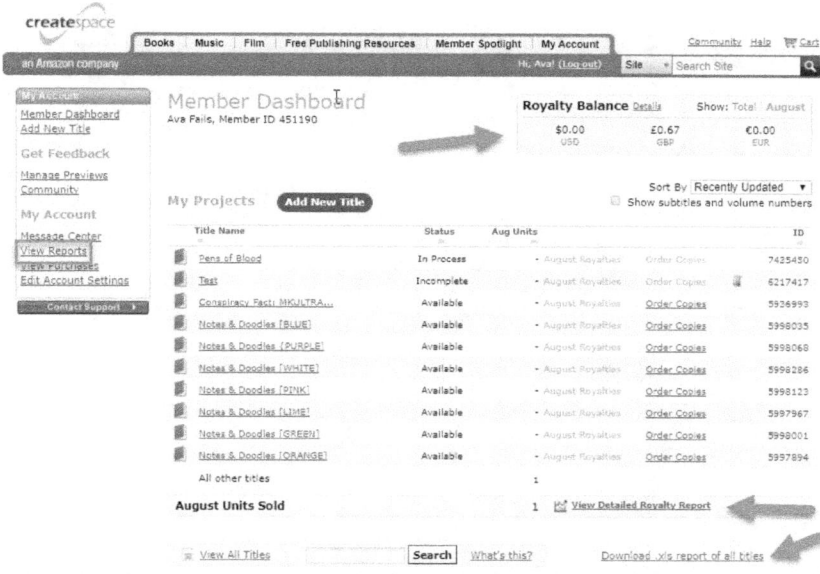

Step 2. Click **View Reports** in the left navigation.

Here you can view and download a variety of reports, so have a look around and check it out.

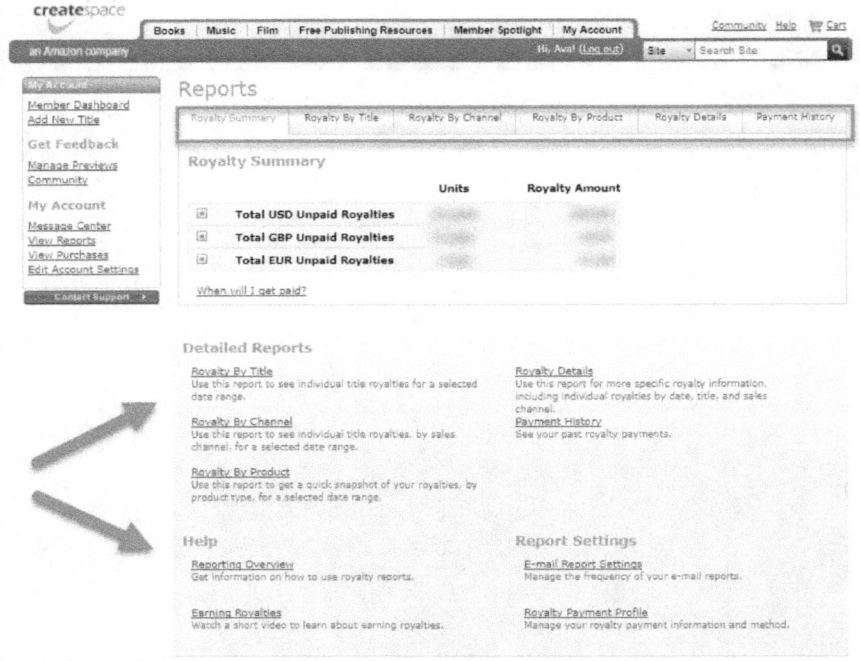

There are also help topics available here to better help you understand what your looking at.

What You Should Expect for Tax Time

Amazon sends you a 1099 form at the end of the year. You will be responsible for paying taxes on your earnings when you file your Tax Returns. It's a smart idea to save around a third of your earnings to cover this cost.

This is probably my least favorite subject matter when it comes to self-publishing. I really don't obsess over this stuff at all. I let it be what it is and do my thing as a writer.

That being said, I can't offer an effective series of tutorials without telling you how to get paid, so there you have it!

Marketing Your Book

As a self-published author, not only are you your own publishing company, but you are also responsible for marketing your book.

Unfortunately, you can't just throw it out there, sit back, and collect the cash...at least not at first. You have to get over the hurdle of building that initial following.

If your niche is hot, this will be easier than if you have focused on a tighter or more popular niche.

Examples From My Experience

I published my first book in 2011. In 2015, I came across a fella on YouTube named Jason Bracht. This guy was making money in self-publishing hand over fist...to the tune of $10,000 a month. Needless to say, I was intrigued.

Hot Niche

Around that same time, I found another guy on the Warrior Forum (no link; it's just an Internet Marketing forum in decline) who was giving away a blueprint for making bank with cookbooks.

I'm no cook, and don't even care about it much, but this seemed simply enough, so I thought I'd give cookbooks a try.

I was doing low carb at the time, so I decided to focus there. My first book did really well. It hit #1 on both the free and paid lists.

Free:

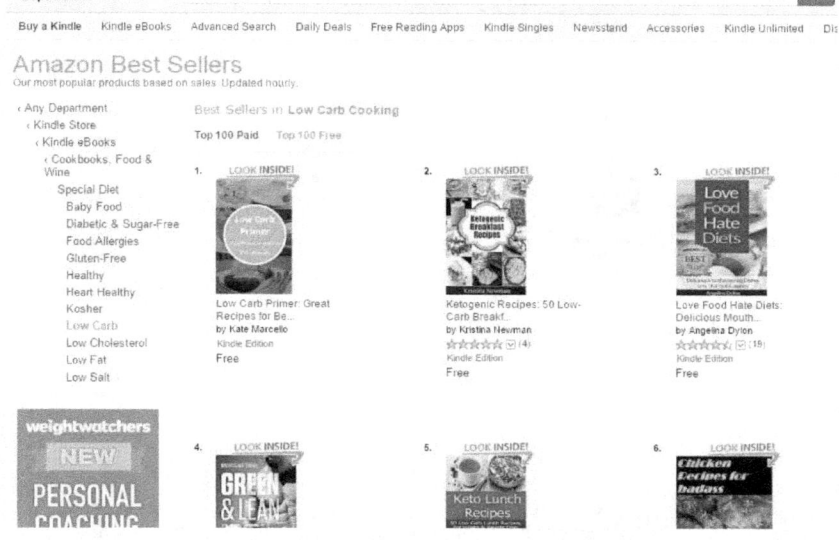

Paid:

SELF-PUBLISHING ON A ZERO BUDGET

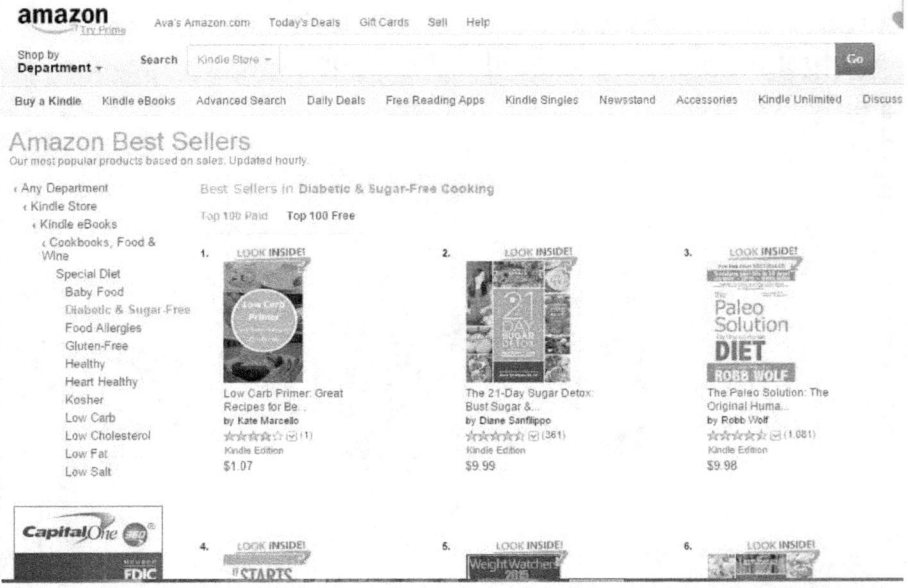

I thought I'd found my path to being the next $10,000 per month earner.
I immediately started writing the second one and this is where I issue a warning.

WARNING
Recipes are sort of a gray area. They are considered a list of facts which cannot be copyrighted. This is NOT a loophole and I mistakenly used it as such. While I did NOT copy and paste the recipes into my book, I did use recipes that I collected from the Internet. Even though I changed the names of them and wrote the procedure for making the dish in my own words, I still got spanked for copyright infringement. My second book was pulled from Amazon.

I quit cookbooks.

I figured it was best to stick to what I know and to use my own thoughts and words all the way. I impress upon you to do the same.

Not-So-Hot Niche

I have books in the memoir niche, ADHD, self-publishing, and teen fiction. These books do okay. They would probably do better if I concentrated a little more on what I'm teaching you here.

My best niche is conspiracy theories which makes me consistent money EVERY month.

What is the Goal of Your Book?

What is the goal you want to accomplish with your book?

Are you in it for the money? If so, you'll want to go after a hot niche.

If you're in it because it's your passion, write and publish that!

Marketing Elements to Include in Your Manuscript

1. Clean manuscript - This is your first line to greatness. Make sure your manuscript is error-free. We talked

about doing this on a ZERO budget in **Part 2 of this series**.
2. Title - Does your title grab attention? It should.
3. Front and End matter - The front and end matter of your book can often be the same thing. This includes things like your About the Author section where you would mention your other books, links to your website, links to your social media, and a link to your email list opt-in form.
4. Request for reviews - It's completely acceptable to include a reminder to your readers to give your book an honest review. Reviews drive sales.

Marketing Your Book Before and After Launch

Your first fans are always going to be the people you already know like your friends and family. Often there is a fine line between bombarding your network with business stuff and just being social; however, you must start somewhere.

In my experience, your friends and family are a great way to get reviews.
I actually created an email list just for this purpose (Mailchimp is free for up to 2000 subs). Rather than using my social networks to drive sales, I use them to push my free promo. It's not so business-y when they get your book for free. There's billions of other people to sell to.

Creating a Series of books is a great way to expand your reach. This allows you to cross promote your books by placing front and end matter showing the other books in the series into your manuscript.

The Art of the Box Set - I first learned about the box set from Steve Smith of PassionatePages.com. Steve writes erotica which I'm not remotely interested in, but he has some insights on self-publishing that are valuable.
He is the king of selling a story more than once.

For example, he publishes short stories which he sells for 99 cents each.
Once he has a good number like 20 or so, he will publish a box set for $2.99.

Then he will do it again at 50 for $4.99.

Sure, he will have certain fans that buy his stories more than once, but for the most part, he is reaching more readers who get their value from buying the box sets. I thought this was pretty genius.

Steve also said back in 2015 that he was making more money on Google Play Books than from Kindle.

That's why later in this series, I will be showing you how to expand to other platforms including Google Play.

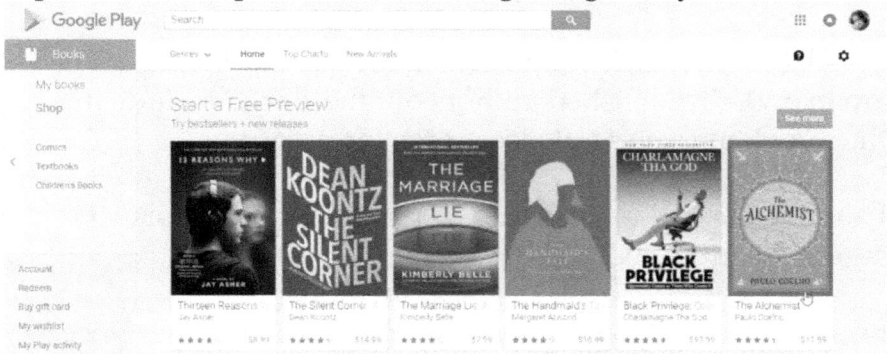

Price your book realistically and strategically. Once you have gone through writing a book and publishing it, you tend to want to value it accordingly.

Realistically, no one is going to pay $25 or even $10 for your ebook. I'm not saying it's never happened, but it is the exception rather than the rule.

Ideally, you want to price your book between $2.99 and $9.99.

Why?

Because this is your 70% royalty range.

If you price it at less, your royalty drops to 35%.

Also, you will garner more sales in this range. Books priced less are seen as mediocre and if they are too expensive, they simply will not sell.

Is a Preorder right for you? Setting your book up for pre-order (or your next one) is a great way to build momentum. It also gets money rollin' in while you are putting the finishing touches on your manuscript. It's just a matter of taste.

Goodreads is a social network for authors and readers. There are many self-published authors out there who include this in their book marketing. It also works for preorders.

I am not one of them. I do have an account, but I just can't seem to want to spend time there.

Be sure to set up your Amazon Author Central page. Once you've published your book to KDP, you can set up your page on **Author Central**.

This is a fairly intuitive process. You will want to have a picture and a bio prepared to add to your page. Then you can search for your books and claim them so they appear on your page.

The link created by your author name on your book sales page will link to this page.

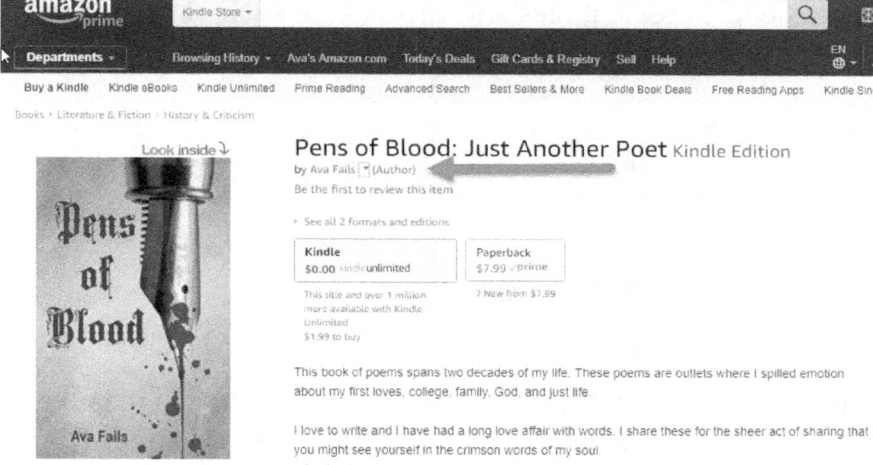

Social Media is one of the best free marketing tools out there. At bare minimum, you should have a Facebook Page and Twitter Profile separate from your personal pages that focuses on you as an author.

I know a lot of people get hung up on Twitter, and it very well may be dying. However, it's still a great place for authors to promote their work with relevant hashtags and more. Here are all of my Twitter tricks FREE.

It's simple to create social media content for your book using Canva. See my post on that here.

Some people create pages and profiles for each of their books. I don't recommend this. You will burn out quickly trying to manage all of that. Create a page and profile for your author name or pen name and market all of your books in one place per social network.

Speaking of Pen Names

If you write in more than one niche, it's a good idea to create a separate pen name for that niche simply so your readers don't get confused.

For example, if you write Romantic Fiction primarily, and you publish a Non-Fiction How-To book on self-publishing, you fiction fan base will most likely not be interested in that title.

Essentially, you will be marketing to the wrong target audience, so it's necessary to create a new audience for that niche.

Benefits of Permafree Books

What is a permafree book?

A permafree book is your book listed free on Amazon.

Why?

Permafree books are a great marketing tool especially for a book series. You can use the free price point to hook readers on the first title and if they like it, they will buy the other books in that series.

You can also use permafree books to promote other parts of your author platform like your website, a video channel, your email list, Steemit...pretty much anything you want to promote.

Permafree books allow you to leverage Amazon and the popularity of your chosen niche.

The Caveat of Permafree

Amazon doesn't allow you to set your book price below 99 cents.
In order to make your book free on Amazon, you have to publish it free on a different online bookseller like Barnes & Noble, Kobo, or Google Play Books.

Then you have to go back to your book listing on Amazon and tell them about a lower price.

Product details

File Size: 1981 KB
Print Length: 75 pages
Publisher: Fill in the Blank Books; 1 edition (July 19, 2017)
Publication Date: July 19, 2017
Sold by: Amazon Digital Services LLC
Language: English
ASIN: B0743MSG6W
Text-to-Speech: Enabled
X-Ray: Not Enabled
Word Wise: Enabled
Lending: Enabled
Screen Reader: Supported
Enhanced Typesetting: Enabled
Amazon Best Sellers Rank: #1,376,668 Paid in Kindle Store (See Top 100 Paid in Kindle Store)
   #3570 in Books > Literature & Fiction > History & Criticism > Genres & Styles > **Poetry**
   #9292 in Kindle Store > Kindle eBooks > Literature & Fiction > History & Criticism > **Criticism & Theory**
   #15064 in Kindle Store > Kindle Short Reads > Two hours or more (65-100 pages) > **Literature & Fiction**

Would you like to tell us about a lower price?

Then it's just a waiting game to see how long it takes them to begin price matching. Even then, your book may not be free in all markets.

Being Active in Your Niche

This is one of the best marketing tools in your arsenal.

This is why I always advise writing on something you are passionate about because you will eat, sleep, and breathe the topic if you are doing it right.

Being active in your niche means that you can promote your content on forums and in Groups where you are active without being seen as only there to sell your book.

There are Facebook Groups, Reddit Subreddits, and all kinds of other places where you can list your book free, but the problem with these places if that there is no reader audience. There are only other authors trying to promote their books. I don't recommend even wasting time here.

You will do much better if you are involved in your niche and can naturally promote in places that you regularly contribute.

Your Author Website

In this day and age, I shouldn't have to explain to you why you need your own website. It's such a low-cost investment for a place that is all yours. If Facebook, Steemit, Twitter, or even Amazon blew up tomorrow, you'd still have your website.

You don't necessarily have to sell from your website, but you certainly can. Just be sure to match your price to Amazon.

You can also use your website to build your audience with email marketing. Your website and email marketing are something that I will certainly cover as we go forward in this series.

If you are considering creating your own website, my recommendation is WordPress.org, hands-down.

Kindle Direct Publishing Marketing Tools

If you enrolled your book in KDP Select, then you have a couple options:

1. **Free Book Promotion** - This option allows you to promote your book as a free download for 5 days out of every 90 you are enrolled in KDP Select.
2. **Kindle Countdown Deal** - This option allows you to create a timed discount where buyers can see how much time is left to get your book at a special price.

I always use the free book promo to offer my book to my friends and family free of charge to get reviews. I can sell to everyone else. I like to run all 5 days at launch.

Paid Marketing

I am only touching on this because it is cheap and effective. It is certainly not required.

Amazon now offers promotion through their ad network. This is cheap, targeting promotion that brings your book up in relevant searches ahead of your competition. You can easily 10x your book sales this way.

You can also do the same with Facebook ads. For as low as $5, you can promote to a highly targeted audience.

This is just a starting point. There are a ton of creative ways to market your books and a lot of information out there on this topic.

Be smart. Spend your time on building assets to your marketing arsenal rather than posting your book link everywhere willy nilly.

That's the End!

There you have it! If you found this book helpful, I'd love to **hear from you**.

If you have questions, I'm happy to answer them.

To see more tutorials, **check out my Steemit blog**.

You can also **check out my other books here**.

Thanks for reading!

www.ingramcontent.com/pod-product-compliance
Lightning Source LLC
Chambersburg PA
CBHW070301230526
45470CB00002B/668